The Times-Picayune

LSU's

2007 championship season

MW00711987

SP
SPORTS PUBLISHING L.L.C.
tsPublishingLLC.com

2007 NATIONAL
CHAMPIONS
LSU TIGERS

Allstate
BCS
NATIONAL
CHAMPIONSHIP
NEW ORLEANS 2008

Collegiate Images
OFFICIALLY LICENSED

back on top

The Times-Picayune

Designed by Adrianna Garcia
Edited by Richard Russell and Michael J. Montalbano

Sports editor: Doug Tatum
Photo editor: Doug Parker
Photographers: Chuck Cook, Rusty Costanza, Michael DeMocker, Chris Granger, David Grunfeld, Eliot Kamenitz, Ted Jackson, John McCusker
Photo imaging: Joseph Graham and Alexander Maillho
Contributing writers: James Varney, Peter Finney, John DeShazier
Design director: George Berke

Managing editor/news: Dan Shea

Sports Publishing LLC

Publisher: Peter L. Bannon
Senior managing editors: Susan M. Moyer
Coordinating editor: Noah A. Amstadter
Art director: Dustin Hubbart

Copyright © 2008, The Times-Picayune LLC

No part of this book may be reproduced in any form or by an electronic or mechanical means including information storage and retrieval systems — except in the case of brief quotations embodied in critical articles or reviews — without permission in writing from its publisher, Sports Publishing LLC.

All stories and photographs are from the files of The Times-Picayune unless otherwise noted.

All identifying marks of LSU are trademarks of LSU. All rights reserved.

All photographs from the 2008 BCS Championship Game are licensed by Collegiate Images on behalf of the BCS. All rights reserved.

Hardcover ISBN: 978-1-59670-303-2
Softcover ISBN: 978-1-59670-304-9

Cover photo by Eliot Kamenitz.
Back cover photo by Chuck Cook.

CONTENTS

Few of the LSU faithful disagreed with quarterback Matt Flynn as he gestured to fans while walking off the field after LSU defeated defending national champion Florida on Oct. 6th in Baton Rouge.
STAFF PHOTO BY CHUCK COOK

miss. state

LSU linebacker Darry Beckwith, top, and safety Craig Steltz, bottom, bring down Mississippi State running back Anthony Dixon, showing the Tigers were ready for business. STAFF PHOTO BY CHUCK COOK

TIGERS **45**
BULLDOGS **0**

08.30.07 | 7 p.m. | Davis Wade Stadium | Starkville, Miss.

Safety Craig Steltz intercepts a pass intended for Mississippi State wide receiver Brandon McRae in the second quarter. Steltz accounted for three of the Tigers' six interceptions.
STAFF PHOTO BY CHUCK COOK

tigers 45
bulldogs 0

BY JAMES VARNEY STAFF WRITER

The stifling defense of LSU lived up to its preseason hype, overwhelming Mississippi State as the Tigers took their season opener 45-0 in Starkville, Miss.

Riding six interceptions, three of them by senior safety Craig Steltz, LSU dominated the Bulldogs' offense all night while enjoying favorable field position on many drives. Mississippi State junior quarterback Michael Henig was pounded mercilessly, and a linebacker corps led by senior Ali Highsmith, who had eight tackles, bottled up the run.

So controlling was LSU's defense that it even topped last year's performance against Mississippi State, when the Bulldogs managed 14 net yards rushing in a 48-17 setback to the Tigers. This year, Mississippi State rushed for 10.

The Tigers jumped to a 17-0 lead by halftime and then, after gliding 71 yards down the field on six plays to open the second half, salted the game away on fifth-year senior quarterback Matt Flynn's 12-yard touchdown pass to senior wide receiver Early Doucet.

In truth, however, the outcome was never really in doubt, as LSU's defensive line swarmed over Mississippi State from the opening kickoff.

It was more of the same in the second half.

Sophomore quarterback Ryan Perrilloux led LSU's second unit on two more touchdown drives in the fourth quarter, but those came long after most of the disconsolate 50,112 had trickled out of humidity-drenched Davis Wade Stadium.

Even when not hounded, Henig displayed some of the dubious pocket judgment Mississippi State Coach Sylvester

tigers 45 bulldogs 0

Croom had fretted about during the preseason. Henig threw to receivers blanketed by Tigers cornerbacks, into double coverage deep over the middle and sometimes into zones that seemed occupied only by purple-clad defenders.

Flynn, making his first regular-season start, played well when given time, completing 12 of 19 passes to five receivers for 128 yards and two touchdowns. Eight of those completions were to Doucet, who set a career high with nine catches for 78 yards.

LSU finished with 347 yards of offense to Mississippi State's 146, and the stat sheet reflected other lopsided numbers, too. For example, the Tigers had 22 first downs to the Bulldogs' nine. Some other figures proved more disconcerting to LSU Coach Les Miles, however, leading with the four sacks for 37 yards in losses.

And while LSU senior running back Jacob Hester averaged nearly 5 yards per carry (finishing with 68 yards on 14 carries), the Tigers repeatedly ran it up the gut for no gain. The sweeps the Tigers attempted failed throughout the night, with sophomore wide receiver Trindon Holliday, one of LSU's explosive threats, gaining 19 yards on six carries.

"In the end, we made the plays we need to, so I feel pretty good about it," Flynn said. "But we've got a lot of work to do."

LSU used three tailbacks in the first quarter.

Sophomore tailback Keiland Williams scored on two 1-run yards, and Perrilloux scored on a 3-yard run. Touchdown passes to Doucet and sophomore running back Charles Scott from Flynn, and another from Perrilloux to sophomore wide receiver Brandon LaFell, rounded out the Tigers' end-zone visits.

LSU junior Colt David was perfect on extra points and opened the scoring with a 27-yard field goal.

The Tigers repeatedly were flagged for false starts, finishing with eight penalties for 60 yards. Some of those miscues could be chalked up to opening-game jitters, but it hardly mattered in the end because there was never any question about whether its defense was in command.

TEAM	1ST	2ND	3RD	4TH	FINAL
LSU	3	14	14	14	45
Mississippi State	0	0	0	0	0

Attendance 50,112 at Davis-Wade Stadium

SCORING SUMMARY

LSU	Colt David 27-yard field goal. Seven plays, 35 yards in 2:16.
LSU	Keiland Williams 1-yard run (David kick). Eight plays, 38 yards in 2:38.
LSU	Williams 1-yard run (David kick). Seven plays, 41 yards in 1:30.
LSU	Early Doucet 11-yard pass from Matt Flynn (David kick). Six plays, 73 yards in 2:01.
LSU	Charles Scott 11-yard pass from Flynn (David kick). Two plays, 8 yards in 0:40.
LSU	Ryan Perrilloux 3-yard run (David kick). Nine plays, 45 yards in 5:21.
LSU	Brandon LaFell 15-yard pass from Perrilloux (David kick). Two plays, 36 yards in 0:29.

TEAM STATISTICS

	LSU	MISS STATE
FIRST DOWNS	22	9
RUSHES-YARDS (NET)	50-198	26-10
PASSING YARDS (NET)	149	136
PASSES (ATT-COMP-INT)	22-14-0	33-14-6
TOTAL OFFENSE (PLAYS-YARDS)	72-347	59-146
PENALTIES (NUMBER-YARDS)	8-60	7-39
PUNTS (NUMBER-AVERAGE)	7-44.9	5-35.6
PUNT RETURNS (NUMBER-YARDS-TD)	1-5-0	4-18-0
KICKOFF RETURNS (NUMBER-YARDS-TD)	1-26-0	7-131-0
POSSESSION TIME	32:45	27:15
SACKS BY (YARDS LOST)	4-37	3-19
FIELD GOALS (ATTEMPTED-MADE)	1-1	0-0
FUMBLES-LOST	0-0	3-1

INDIVIDUAL OFFENSIVE STATISTICS

RUSHING LSU — Jacob Hester 14-68; Matt Flynn 11-42; Richard Murphy 6-35; Trindon Holliday 6-19; Keiland Williams 7-18; Ryan Perrilloux 3-12. MISS STATE — Anthony Dixon 13-29; Justin Williams 4-10; Christian Ducre 1-2; Wesley Carroll 3 minus-6; Michael Henig 4 minus-22.

PASSING LSU — Matt Flynn 19/12-2-0, 128; Ryan Perrilloux 3/2-1-0, 21. MISS STATE — Michael Henig 28/11-0-6, 120; Wesley Carroll 5/3-0-0, 16.

RECEIVING LSU — Early Doucet 9-78; Terrance Toliver 1-19; Chris Mitchell 1-16; Brandon LaFell 1-15; Charles Scott 1-11; Jacob Hester 1-10. MISS STATE — Arnil Stallworth 3-33; Lance Long 2-16; Christian Ducre 2-2.

INDIVIDUAL DEFENSIVE STATISTICS

INTERCEPTIONS LSU — Craig Steltz 3; Danny McCray 1; Curtis Taylor 1; Jonathan Zenon 1.

SACKS LSU — Glenn Dorsey 1; Lazarius Levingston 1; Danny McCray 1; Al Woods 1. MISS STATE — Titus Brown 1; Dominic Douglas 1; Jimmie Holmes 1.

TACKLES LSU — Ali Highsmith 8; Glenn Dorsey 5; Harry Coleman 4; Jonathan Zenon 4. MISS STATE — Dominic Douglas 9; Anthony Johnson 8.

ap top 10 released 09.02.07

LSU's Jacob Hester, right, and others congratulate tailback Keiland Williams after a second-quarter touchdown, Williams' second against the Bulldogs.
STAFF PHOTO BY CHUCK COOK

1 USC
First-place votes: 59

2 LSU
First-place votes: 5

3 WEST VIRGINIA

4 FLORIDA

5 OKLAHOMA

5 WISCONSIN

7 TEXAS

8 LOUISVILLE

9 VIRGINIA TECH

10 CAL

va. tech

TIGERS 48
HOKIES 7

09.08.07 | 8:15 p.m. | Tiger Stadium | Baton Rouge, La.

Kirston Pittman (49) leads the charge for the Tigers against Hokies tailback Brandon Ore in the second quarter. Under a relentless attack by LSU's defense, the Hokies finished with only 149 yards on offense.
STAFF PHOTO BY CHUCK COOK

tigers 48
hokies 7

BY JAMES VARNEY STAFF WRITER

SO much for sluggish.

Five days after LSU Coach Les Miles apparently invented the phrase "wantango offense," he unleashed something like it on No. 9 Virginia Tech in a crushing 48-7 win.

The No. 2-ranked Tigers (2-0) scored early and late, on repeated long drives and with quick strikes.

LSU overwhelmed Virginia Tech (1-1) in every statistical category and did not allow the Hokies across midfield until deep into the third quarter. That kind of performance erased some of the sour memories fans nursed over LSU's first-half production against Mississippi State the previous week in Starkville, Miss.

LSU's rout of Virginia Tech was the worst in Hokies Coach Frank Beamer's career since a 45-0 drubbing by Vanderbilt in 1982.

LSU sent a message, racking up nearly 600 yards in offense and six touchdowns against a Virginia Tech team that led the nation in total defense the past two seasons. The Tigers converted third downs seemingly at will and blended rushes and passes in a way that kept Hokies defenders guessing.

As a result of that balanced attack, LSU had three running backs averaging more than 6 yards a carry, including sophomore Keiland Williams, who gained 126 yards on seven carries, with touchdown scampers of 67 and 32 yards. The Tigers' offense also featured a breakout performance from sophomore wide receiver Brandon LaFell, who finished with a career-best six catches for 125 yards.

"We were surprised we dominated them like that, because

Quarterback Matt Flynn, scoring on a 7-yard run against Virginia Tech in the first quarter, and LSU roared out of the gate in a highly anticipated matchup of top 10 teams that was lopsided from the start. STAFF PHOTO BY CHUCK COOK

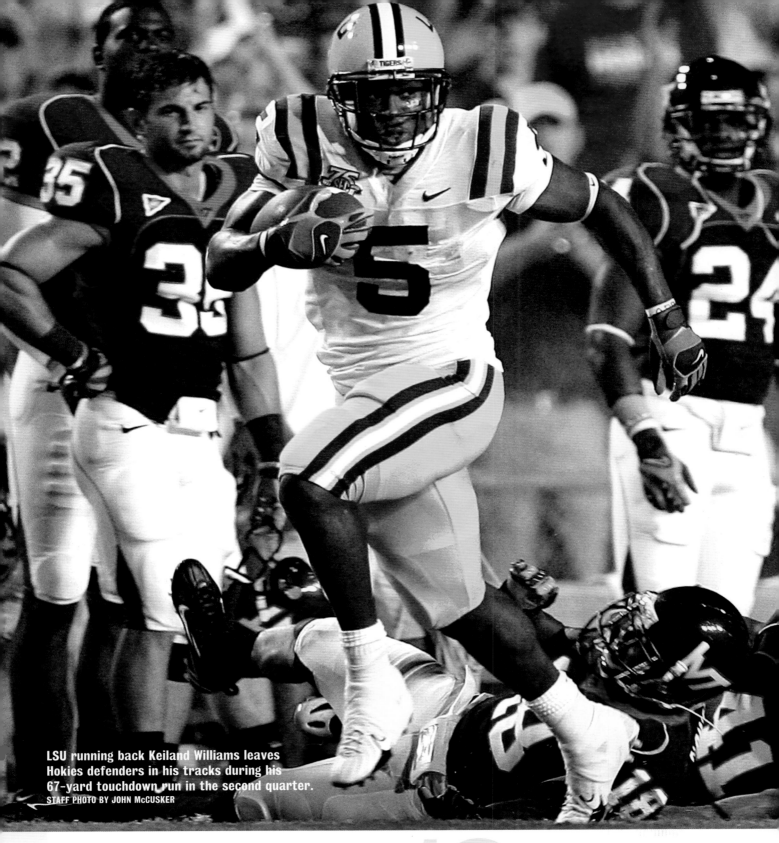

LSU running back Keiland Williams leaves
Hokies defenders in his tracks during his
67-yard touchdown run in the second quarter.
STAFF PHOTO BY JOHN McCUSKER

ap top 10
released 09.09.07

tigers 48 | hokies 7

they have a great team," LSU senior running back Jacob Hester said. "We just got off to a really good start and held on."

Hester had nothing but praise for the Hokies, who were playing their first season after 32 people were killed on the Blacksburg, Va., campus, in April. But Hester also offered one terrifying tidbit for future LSU opponents this season.

"We wanted to show we are more than just a defensive team," he said, noting he believes there is still room for improvement in the Tigers' offense.

Meanwhile, when Virginia Tech had the ball, LSU's defense was smothering. Virginia Tech mustered 40 yards in offense on 26 first-half snaps and ended with 149 yards.

Starting junior quarterback Sean Glennon failed to make it to halftime. He was replaced in the second quarter by freshman Tyrod Taylor, and their main rushing threat, junior tailback Brandon Ore, endured a miserable effort, averaging 2.5 yards per carry.

Even the Hokies' vaunted special teams, a signature under Beamer, were outshone by LSU. Although LSU senior punter Patrick Fisher had two outstanding kicks that were wiped out by penalties, he averaged nearly 45 yards.

Even in those rare moments when Virginia Tech appeared to get a spark, it immediately fizzled. Time and again the Hokies ran plays for positive yardage, then got stuffed or tossed incomplete passes. Virginia Tech finished with eight punts.

The result also was very different from the last non-Southeastern Conference matchup of Top 10 teams at Tiger Stadium, a 13-13 tie against Ohio State in 1987.

Against the Hokies, the decision came quickly and decisively.

LSU scored first — and took control of the game — early on a pair of 80-yard-plus drives in the first quarter. The first,

1 USC
First-place
votes: 40

2 LSU
First-place
votes: 25

3 OKLAHOMA

4 WEST
VIRGINIA

5 FLORIDA

6 TEXAS

7 WISCONSIN

8 CAL

9 LOUISVILLE

10 OHIO
STATE

tigers 48 hokies 7

after the opening kickoff, covered 87 yards and ended with Hester plunging in from the 3-yard line one play after Flynn and he combined on a shovel pass that went for 28 yards.

The second, an 85-yarder, was highlighted by a square-in route on which Flynn found LaFell on a dead run, and LaFell took it 56 yards to Virginia Tech's 25-yard line. The Tigers then faced two third-and-6 situations. LSU converted the first, and Flynn scampered on the second for 7 yards and a touchdown.

His run clearly fooled the Hokies' defense, after LSU sent three receivers wide left and then Flynn ran right, side-stepped a Virginia Tech linebacker at the 5 and went in unscathed.

After senior Craig Steltz stepped in front of Glennon's slant-in pass — Steltz's fourth interception of the season, equaling his total for all of last season — junior Colt David made a 30-yard field goal in the second quarter.

Williams completed the first-half rout, taking a pitch right from Flynn, vaulting over a sprawling Hokie, then taking off down the sideline on a 67-yard scoring run that ended with Williams veering back across the field to the corner of the end zone in front of LSU's student section.

In the second half, although Taylor's mobility produced a spark for the Hokies and led to their only touchdown — the first the Tigers' defense has surrendered this season — it was more misery for Virginia Tech.

David made another field goal, this time from 28 yards, and sophomore backup quarterback Ryan Perrilloux connected with senior wide receiver Early Doucet for a 34-yard touchdown pass. That play came after Flynn had also hit Doucet with a long pass on third down to set up the Tigers with a first down at Virginia Tech's 34-yard line.

TEAM	1ST	2ND	3RD	4TH	FINAL
Virginia Tech	0	0	7	0	7
LSU	14	10	10	14	48

Attendance 92,739 at Tiger Stadium

SCORING SUMMARY

LSU	Jacob Hester 3-yard run (Colt David kick). Ten plays, 87 yards in 4:14.
LSU	Matt Flynn 7-yard run (David kick). Eight plays, 85 yards in 3:06.
LSU	David 30-yard field goal. Four plays, 7 yards in 1:30.
LSU	Keiland Williams 67-yard run (David kick). One play, 67 yards in 0:15.
LSU	David 28-yard field goal. Ten plays, 45 yards in 4:45.
VA TECH	Tyrod Taylor 1-yard run (Jud Dunlevy). Eight plays, 65 yards in 3:42.
LSU	Early Doucet 34-yard pass from Ryan Perrilloux (David kick). Six plays, 76 yards in 2:54.
LSU	Williams 32-yard run (David kick). Eight plays, 87 yards in 4:20.
LSU	Terrance Toliver 28-yard pass from Perrilloux (David kick) Nine plays, 94 yards in 4:25.

TEAM STATISTICS

	LSU	VA TECH
FIRST DOWNS	28	11
RUSHES-YARDS (NET)	41-297	28-71
PASSINGS YARDS (NET)	301	78
PASSES (ATT-COMP-INT)	32-22-0	29-9-1
TOTAL OFFENSE (PLAYS-YARDS)	73-598	57-149
PENALTIES (NUMBER-YARDS)	7-62	7-65
PUNTS (NUMBER-AVERAGE)	3-44.7	8-40.1
PUNT RETURNS (NUMBER-YARDS-TD)	0-0-0	1-1-0
KICKOFF RETURNS (NUMBER-YARDS-TD)	2-21-0	9-177-0
POSSESSION TIME	34:33	25:27
SACKS BY (YARDS LOST)	3-22	2-2
FIELD GOALS (ATTEMPTED-MADE)	2-2	0-0
FUMBLES-LOST	0-0	1-0

INDIVIDUAL OFFENSIVE STATISTICS

RUSHING LSU — Keiland Williams 7-126; Jacob Hester 12-81; Trindon Holliday 4-32; Charles Scott 4-24; Ryan Perrilloux 4-21; Matt Flynn 7-12; Richard Murphy 2-2.
VA TECH — Tyrod Taylor 9-44; Branden Ore 14-28; Sean Glennon 2-2.

PASSING LSU — Matt Flynn 27/17-0-0, 217; Ryan Perrilloux 5/5-2-0, 84
VA TECH — Tyrod Taylor 18/7-0-0, 62; Sean Glennon 10/2-0-1; Eddie Royal 1/0-0-0, 16.

RECEIVING LSU — Brandon LaFell 7-125; Early Doucet 6-75; Demetrius Byrd 2-22; Keiland Williams 2-10; Jacob Hester 1-28; Terrance Toliver 1-28; Charles Scott 1-11; Trindon Holliday 1-3; Jared Mitchell 1 minus-1.
VA TECH — Josh Morgan 4-20; Branden Ore 2-24; Chris Drager 1-14; Justin Harper 1-11.

INDIVIDUAL DEFENSIVE STATISTICS

INTERCEPTIONS LSU — Craig Steltz 1.

SACKS LSU — Rahim Alem 1-0; Craig Steltz 1-0; Curtis Taylor 1-0.
VA TECH — Xavier Adibi 1; team 1.

TACKLES LSU — Kirston Pittman 8; Danny McCray 7; Glenn Dorsey 6; Ali Highsmith 6; Darry Beckwith 4; Perry Riley 4; Craig Steltz 4.
VA TECH — D.J. Parker 11; Brandon Flowers 9; Xavier Adibi 9; Kam Chancellor 9; Vince Hall 8.

The Tigers' Brandon LaFell, who caught seven passes for 125 yards, finds plenty of room against Virginia Tech in the first quarter.
STAFF PHOTO BY CHUCK COOK

middle tenn.

LSU defensive end
Tyson Jackson reaches
out to break up a
pass by Middle Tennessee
State quarterback
Joe Craddock.
STAFF PHOTO BY JOHN McCUSKER

The Blue Raiders' Joe Craddock feels the heat from Tigers safety Danny McCray. Craddock completed six of 11 passes for 59 yards, and he was sacked four times.
STAFF PHOTO BY JOHN McCUSKER

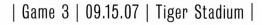

| Game 3 | 09.15.07 | Tiger Stadium |

tigers 44
blue raiders 0

BY JAMES VARNEY STAFF WRITER

Another game, another rout for LSU.

The No. 2-ranked Tigers dispatched Middle Tennessee State 44-0 in workmanlike fashion in Baton Rouge. The game was pretty much over when LSU led 3-0, as it became obvious the overmatched Blue Raiders from the Sun Belt Conference could do zip offensively, and for many fans that made perhaps the most intriguing aspect of the game figuring out who would play for the Tigers (3-0).

LSU Coach Les Miles substituted liberally throughout, giving valuable game experience to many younger players. Not all of his personnel cycling was attributable to the blowout. In some cases injuries forced his hand.

Most notably, fifth-year senior quarterback Matt Flynn did not play a down. Flynn, suffering from a high ankle sprain, suited up for the game, both feet swathed in so much tape it looked like he was wearing winter boots. Senior wide receiver Early Doucet, on the other hand, was not in pads. He reportedly suffered a groin pull in practice leading up to the game.

Sophomore Ryan Perrilloux started in Flynn's place and had a huge performance. After LSU receivers dropped his first two passes, Perrilloux completed 20 of his next 23 passes, finishing with 298 yards and three touchdowns in less than three quarters of work. The scoring passes brought his season total to six. He also scrambled effectively, often on third down, including one 11-yard gain that ended with him diving forward for the last 2 yards to get a first down.

In the second quarter, Perrilloux produced the game's most sensational play, a 62-yard scoring pass to junior wide receiver Demetrius Byrd that came after Middle Tennessee State had failed on a fourth-down attempt just inside LSU territory.

tigers 44 | blue raiders 0

For the Blue Raiders, the game marked the second consecutive loss on the road to a Top 10 team.

After taking a 23-0 halftime lead, LSU poured it on in the third quarter, scoring three touchdowns. The first touchdown came on a double-pitch reverse to sophomore wide receiver Brandon LaFell who, with Perrilloux leading the blocking out in the flat, raced down the sideline 18 yards for a score.

After sophomore defensive end Rahim Alem forced a Middle Tennessee State fumble and sophomore safety Harry McCray fell on the ball at the Blue Raiders' 15-yard line, LSU needed one play to make the score 37-0. Perrilloux dropped back, spotted freshman wide receiver Terrance Toliver behind a seam in the middle of the end zone, and delivered him the ball under the goal posts. Toliver took a hard shot but held on for the score.

The third touchdown came on an 8-yard run by redshirt freshman Richard Murphy. The run came after Perrilloux had, beginning on a second-and-18 in LSU territory, connected with sophomore running back Keiland Williams and LaFell on back-to-back passes that picked up 30 yards. Sophomore wide receiver Jared Mitchell also got into the act, taking a short pass over the middle and breaking several tackles as he angled for the sideline and gained 32 yards.

Meanwhile, it was another stellar performance for LSU's defense. Middle Tennessee State punted seven times and failed on two fourth-down attempts. Overall, the Blue Raiders gained 9 yards on 37 carries and had nine first downs.

LSU's defensive line, led by another rock-solid performance from senior tackle Glenn Dorsey, created one nightmare after another for junior quarterback Joe Craddock.

In his last game, Craddock had a career performance against No. 8 Louisville in a high-scoring loss, but he had a very different experience against the Tigers. Running for his life on many plays, he completed six of 11 passes for 59 yards and was sacked four times.

TEAM	1ST	2ND	3RD	4TH	FINAL
Middle Tennessee	0	0	0	0	0
LSU	10	13	21	0	44

Attendance 92,407 at Tiger Stadium

SCORING SUMMARY

LSU — Colt David 29-yard field goal. Twelve plays, 64 yards in 4:24.
LSU — Charles Scott 13-yard pass from Ryan Perrilloux. Twelve plays, 80 yards in 5:02.
LSU — Demetrius Byrd 62-yard pass from Perrilloux. One play, 62 yards in 0:12.
LSU — David 35-yard field goal. Eight plays, 38 yards in 3:07.
LSU — David 26-yard field goal. Eight plays, 50 yards in 1:48.
LSU — Brandon LaFell 18-yard run. Nine plays, 65 yards in 4:01.
LSU — Terrance Toliver 15-yard pass from Perrilloux. One play, 15 yards in 0:07.
LSU — Richard Murphy 8-yard run. Eight plays, 68 yards in 4:52.

TEAM STATISTICS

	LSU	MTSU
FIRST DOWNS	26	9
RUSHES-YARDS	40-198	37-9
PASSING YARDS (NET)	307	81
PASSES (ATT-COMP-INT)	28-21-1	15-8-0
TOTAL OFFENSE (PLAYS-YARDS)	68-505	52-90
PENALTIES (NUMBER-YARDS)	10-58	3-20
PUNTS (NUMBER-AVERAGE)	1-41.0	8-37.4
PUNT RETURNS (NUMBER-YARDS-TD)	2-10-0	0-0-0
KICKOFF RETURNS (NUMBER-YARDS-TD)	1-24-0	7-119-0
POSSESSION TIME	28:51	31:09
SACKS BY (YARDS LOST)	6-58	2-15
FIELD GOALS (ATTEMPTED-MADE)	3-3	0-0
FUMBLES-LOST	0-0	0-0

INDIVIDUAL STATISTICS

RUSHING — LSU — Jacob Hester 10-57; Ryan Perrilloux 8-37; Keiland Williams 5-30; Andrew Hatch 4-27; Brandon LaFell 1-18; Charles Scott 3-17.
MTSU — Dwight Dasher 12-30; DeMarco McNair 8-8; Phillip Tanner 6-2.

PASSING — LSU — Ryan Perrilloux 25/20-3-1, 298; Andrew Hatch 2/1-0-0.
MTSU — Joe Craddock 11/6-0-0, 59; Dwight Dasher 4/2-0-0, 22.

RECEIVING — LSU — Jared Mitchell 6-82; Brandon LaFell 3-47; Charles Scott 3-22; Demetrius Byrd 2-86; Richard Dickson 2-20; Terrance Toliver 1-15.
MTSU — DeMarco McNair 2-25; Patrick Honeycutt 2-21; Wes Caldwell 1-19.

INDIVIDUAL DEFENSIVE STATISTICS

INTERCEPTIONS — MTSU — Dana Stewart 1.
SACKS — LSU — Danny McCray 2; Glenn Dorsey 1; Kirston Pittman 1; Darry Beckwith 0.5; Ali Highsmith 0.5; Perry Riley 0.5; Luke Sanders 0.5.
MTSU — Gary Tucker 1; Andrew Harrington 1.
TACKLES — LSU — Ali Highsmith 7; Darry Beckwith 6; Perry Riley 5; Charles Alexander 4; Lazarius Levingston 4; Craig Steltz 4; Danny McCray 4; Kirston Pittman 4.
MTSU — Andrew Harrington 8; Jeremy Kellem 6; Danny Carmichael 5.

ap top 10 released 09.16.07

Quarterback Ryan Perrilloux completed 20 of 25 passes with three touchdowns and an interception. STAFF PHOTO BY JOHN McCUSKER

1 USC
First-place votes: 46

2 LSU
First-place votes: 19

3 FLORIDA

4 OKLAHOMA

5 WEST VIRGINIA

6 CAL

7 TEXAS

8 OHIO STATE

9 WISCONSIN

10 PENN STATE

TIGERS

GAMECOCKS

28

16

09.22.07 | 2:30 p.m. | Tiger Stadium | Baton Rouge, La.

LSU running back Jacob Hester bullies his way past South Carolina defenders for extra yards.
STAFF PHOTO BY JOHN McCUSKER

tigers
gamecocks

28
16

BY JAMES VARNEY STAFF WRITER

T he record reflected that No. 2 LSU defeated No. 12 South Carolina 28-16 in Baton Rouge, but in truth it was seven points by one player that made the difference.

Junior kicker Colt David scored on a marvelous fake field-goal attempt, then kicked the extra point with just more than a minute left in the first half, making the score 21-7 and essentially driving a stake through the heart of the Gamecocks.

The play was worth a touchdown on style alone. In particular, it was the no-look flip over the shoulder by the holder, fifth-year senior quarterback Matt Flynn, to a streaking David that made the play so memorable.

"It's my first touchdown," a still-beaming David said of his 15-yard run. "My first thought was not to slip. I just didn't want to slip taking off. After that, I just had faith in everyone else to make the blocks."

Aside from that play, however, LSU (4-0, 2-0 Southeastern Conference) looked almost mortal at times. Once again, the key to LSU's victory was a tremendous defensive effort that, despite yielding more than twice as many points as it had all season, showed again that it nearly was impossible to run against.

South Carolina finished with 17 yards on 27 carries, a meager production that reflected three LSU sacks for 26 yards in losses.

LSU Coach Les Miles attributed much of the Tigers' at times shaky execution to the less-than-ideal conditions, as the game unfolded under periodically heavy rain.

South Carolina (3-1, 1-1) was never really in the game, even though the stat sheet showed the Gamecocks put up the best

Kicker Colt David scores on a 15-yard touchdown run off a fake field-goal attempt after holder Matt Flynn used a no-look flip that sent the crowd into a frenzy.
STAFF PHOTO BY JOHN McCUSKER

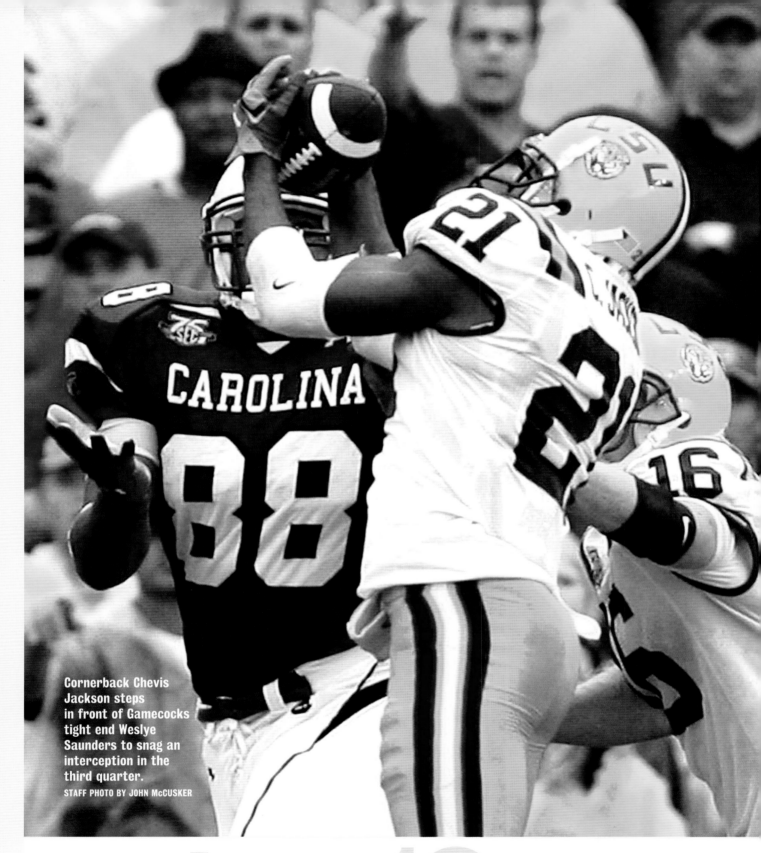

Cornerback Chevis Jackson steps in front of Gamecocks tight end Weslye Saunders to snag an interception in the third quarter.
STAFF PHOTO BY JOHN McCUSKER

ap top 10
released 09.23.07

TEAM	1ST	2ND	3RD	4TH	FINAL
South Carolina	7	0	0	9	16
LSU	7	14	7	0	28

Attendance — 92,530 at Tiger Stadium

SCORING SUMMARY

S.C. Mike Davis 1-yard run (Ryan Succop kick). Twelve 12 plays, 67 yards in 5:52.

LSU Trindon Holliday 33-yard run (Colt David kick). Four plays, 69 yards in 1:23.

LSU Richard Dickson 1-yard pass from Matt Flynn (David kick). Nine plays, 56 yards in 2:55.

LSU David 15-yard run (David kick). Five plays, 32 yards in 2:35.

LSU Jacob Hester 9-yard run (David kick). Five plays, 30 yards in 2:16.

S.C. Succop 23-yard field goal. Eleven plays, 56 yards in 2:44.

S.C. Kenny McKinley 1-yard pass from Chris Smelley (two-point conversion attempt failed). Ten plays, 80 yards in 3:19.

TEAM STATISTICS

TEAM STATISTICS	LSU	S.C.
FIRST DOWNS	19	16
RUSHES-YARDS (NET)	50-290	27-17
PASSING YARDS (NET)	70	244
PASSES (ATT-COMP-INT)	20-8-81	42-19-2
TOTAL OFFENSE (PLAYS-YARDS)	70-360	69-261
PENALTIES (NUMBER-YARDS)	5-39	2-20
PUNTS (NUMBER-AVERAGE)	7-267	5-224
PUNT RETURNS (NUMBER-YARDS-TD)	2-9-0	1-19-0
KICKOFF RETURNS (NUMBER-YARDS-TD)	3-50-0	5-122-0
POSSESSION TIME	32:51	27:09
SACKS BY (YARDS LOST)	3-26	1-6
FIELD GOALS (ATTEMPTED-MADE)	1-0	1-1
FUMBLES-LOST	3-0	2-1

INDIVIDUAL OFFENSIVE STATISTICS

RUSHING LSU — Jacob Hester 17-88; Trindon Holliday 6-73; Ryan Perrilloux 8-59; Keiland Williams 7-33; Colt David 1-15; Richard Murphy 3-15.
S.C. — Cory Boyd 18-17; Kenny McKinley 2-16; Mike Davis 4-10.

PASSING LSU — Matt Flynn 19/8-1-1, 70; Ryan Perrilloux 1/0-0-0, 0.
S.C. — Chris Smelley 26/12-1-1, 174; Blake Mitchell 16/7-0-1, 70.

RECEIVING LSU — Richard Dickson 4-39; Brandon LaFell 2-16; Quinn Johnson 1-9.
S.C. — Kenny McKinley 6-25; Cory Boyd 4-66; Weslye Saunders 4-32; Mike Davis 3-77; Moe Brown 1-27; Jared Cook 1-17.

INDIVIDUAL DEFENSIVE STATISTICS

INTERCEPTIONS LSU — Chevis Jackson 1-0; Danny McCray 1-0.
S.C. — Chris Hampton 1-0.

SACKS LSU — Darry Beckwith 1; Glenn Dorsey 1.
S.C. — Eric Norwood 1-0.

TACKLES LSU — Danny McCray 11; Ali Highsmith 10; Glenn Dorsey 8; Jonathan Zenon 7; Craig Steltz 7.
S.C. — Emanuel Cook 11; Eric Norwood 8; Rodney Paulk 7.

| Game 4 | 09.22.07 | Tiger Stadium |

tigers 28 gamecocks 16

fight of any team yet against LSU, and South Carolina became the first to hold a lead (7-0 in the first quarter) over the Tigers.

The Gamecocks had several plays for long yardage, usually throwing back in the precise zone a Tiger had left or on throws to running backs on crossing patterns who had gotten a step on LSU linebackers. South Carolina punted fewer times than LSU and converted 50 percent of its third-down attempts.

At the same time — and more critically — the Gamecocks were 0-for-2 on two fourth-down attempts in the second half. The first seemed nothing short of bizarre, with South Carolina trailing by two touchdowns less than midway through the third quarter and facing fourth-and-1 on its 30-yard line.

LSU stuffed that straight-forward run, and five plays later senior running back Jacob Hester scored on a 9-yard touchdown scamper that gave the Tigers a 28-7 lead.

Meanwhile, in addition to their seven punts and third-down futility much of the day, the Tigers seemed to have other problems. For example, the passing attack was spotty at best. Sophomore wide receiver Jared Mitchell dropped two passes on the opening series, and Flynn, returning to action for the first time since spraining an ankle against Virginia Tech two weeks earlier, seemed tentative and inaccurate.

Flynn completed eight of 19 passes for 70 yards with an interception and one touchdown, a 1-yard flick over the middle to sophomore tight end Richard Dickson that gave LSU a 14-7 lead with 12:13 remaining in the second quarter. Sophomore quarterback Ryan Perrilloux, who was becoming a more integral part of the LSU offense each week, attempted one pass — an incompletion in the fourth quarter when the game was settled.

LSU defensive coordinator Bo Pelini said he was pleased with the Tigers' overall effort, even as he and the players regretted allowing two touchdowns.

| 1 USC | 2 LSU | 3 OKLAHOMA | 4 FLORIDA | 5 WEST VIRGINIA | 6 CAL | 7 TEXAS | 8 OHIO STATE | 9 WISCONSIN | 10 RUTGERS |

First-place votes: 43 — First-place votes: 22

TIGERS 34
GREEN WAVE 9

09.29.07 | 11 a.m. | Louisiana Superdome | New Orleans, La.

During the first half, Tulane gave running back Charles Scott and LSU fits. But in the second half, the Tigers and Scott, who scored on runs of 3 and 35 yards, found the going a little easier.
STAFF PHOTO BY CHRIS GRANGER

Undaunted by
the Tigers' No. 2
ranking, the Green
Wave sacked Matt
Flynn four times in
the first half.
STAFF PHOTO BY CHRIS GRANGER

tigers 34
green wave 9

BY JAMES VARNEY STAFF WRITER

IT took much longer than expected for the nation's No. 2-ranked team, but LSU asserted itself in the second half and beat Tulane in the 96th meeting between the schools, 34-9, at the Superdome.

Tigers senior running back Jacob Hester and sophomore running back Charles Scott each rushed for two touchdowns, and junior Colt David made two field goals as LSU (5-0) pushed back the Green Wave (1-3).

Still, the final score seemed improbable.

Tulane played inspired football in the first two quarters, particularly along the defensive line, and only trailed 10-9 entering the third quarter.

LSU fifth-year senior Matt Flynn was sacked four times in the first half, and pressure also led to an intentional grounding and a holding call in the end zone that produced a safety for Tulane.

LSU Coach Les Miles insisted the Tigers remained collected at halftime, despite committing 11 penalties and rushing for minus-11 yards in the first half. Tulane kept the ball for more than 18 minutes in the half and had 126 yards of offense compared to LSU's 127.

Said first-year Tulane coach Bob Toledo: "We took the fight to them. They (Tulane) played a lot better than people gave them credit for. I told them, 'nobody's a six-touchdown favorite. We're not going to let that happen.' We didn't pull it off, but we battled, and I think we gained respect all over the country today."

In some respects, Miles seemed almost pleased that LSU, which hadn't had its back to the wall at any point in this season, had to face the prospect of a dogfight. The Tigers' response was outstanding, he said, after a straightforward and not particularly zealous discussion in the locker room.

tigers 34   green wave 9

The game turned in the final 1:40 before halftime after sophomore Trindon Holliday's 38-yard kick return set the Tigers up at their 44-yard line.

Flynn connected with junior wide receiver Demetrius Byrd for 16 yards for a first down on third-and-14, then hit Chris Mitchell for 16 yards to put the ball at Tulane's 19. A couple of dropped passes later, and David gave LSU the lead for good with a 36-yard field goal with three seconds remaining in the half.

LSU dominated the second half, although it continued to get flagged for penalties (the Tigers finished with 15 for 91 yards). Tulane finished with 227 yards in total offense, largely on the strength of senior running back Matt Forté's, who rushed for 73 yards on 16 carries.

After David's second field goal (33 yards) made the score 13-9, Tulane appeared to have more spark. But that was extinguished when, at the end of two back-to-back strong runs, Forté was stripped of the ball by senior linebacker Luke Sanders, and sophomore defensive lineman Al Woods, in his first career start, recovered the fumble.

That led to Hester's second touchdown, a 1-yard plunge.

Scott became a force in the second half, finishing with 53 yards on six carries, including a 35-yard burst in which he shed three sets of tacklers on his way to the end zone.

"Once I got past the line of scrimmage I pretty much saw it, so I went for it," Scott said, noting he was pleased he helped trigger the turnaround.

Miles repeatedly stressed the character the Tigers showed by shrugging off their sluggish first half and taking control. It was the hallmark of a good team, he said, when facing such a genuine and unexpected challenge, that it pulled itself together, began to dominate, and left with a win.

"I thought the defense played well the entire game, but we relied on them way too much," Miles said. "It wasn't our best game, but I'll take victory."

TEAM	1ST	2ND	3RD	4TH	FINAL
LSU	7	3	10	14	34
Tulane	0	9	0	0	9

Attendance   58,769 at the Superdome

SCORING SUMMARY

LSU — Jacob Hester 3-yard run (Colt David kick). Two plays, 49 yards in 0:41.
TULANE — Safety.
TULANE — Andre Anderson, 5-yard run (Ross Thevenot kick). Eleven plays, 58 yards in 4:11.
LSU — David 36-yard field goal. Nine plays, 37 yards in 1:37.
LSU — David 33-yard field goal. Eleven plays, 54 yards in 6:09.
LSU — Jacob Hester 1-yard run (David kick). Five plays, 48 yards in 2:20.
LSU — Charles Scott 35-yard run (David kick). Eight plays, 76 yards in 3:28.
LSU — Scott 3-yard run (David kick). Four plays, 44 yards in 1:39.

TEAM STATISTICS

	LSU	TULANE
FIRST DOWNS	16	12
RUSHING-YARDS (NET)	38-134	33-88
PASSING YARDS (NET)	257	139
PASSES (ATT-COMP-INT)	32-17-1	32-12-1
TOTAL OFFENSE (PLAYS-YARDS)	70-391	65-227
PENALTIES (NUMBER-YARDS)	15-91	4-23
PUNTS (NUMBER-AVERAGE)	5-46.6	10-38.9
PUNT RETURNS (NUMBER-YARDS-TD)	4-25-0	2-8-0
KICKOFF RETURNS (NUMBER-YARDS-TD)	2-64-0	8-107-0
POSSESSION TIME	31:34	28:26
SACKS BY (YARDS-LOST)	2-13	6-44
FIELD GOALS (ATTEMPTED-MADE)	3-2	0-0
FUMBLES-LOST	1-0	2-2

INDIVIDUAL OFFENSIVE STATISTICS

RUSHING   LSU — Charles Scott 6-53; Richard Murphy 6-35; Jacob Hester 10-33.
TULANE — Matt Forté 16-73; Andre Anderson 7-18; Anthony Scelfo 7-4.

PASSING   LSU — Matt Flynn 29/16-0-1, 258; Ryan Perrilloux 3/1-0-0, minus-1.
TULANE — Anthony Scelfo 26/11-0-1, 117; Kevin Moore 5/1-0-0, 22.

RECEIVING   LSU — Brandon LaFell 4-76; Demetrius Byrd 3-69; Chris Mitchell 3-32; Richard Dickson 2-25; Richard Murphy 2-0; Terrance Toliver 1-38.
TULANE — Gabe Ratcliff 4-55; Brian King 4-32; Matt Forté 1-21; Michael Batiste 1-20; Kenneth Guidroz 1-11; Jeremy McKinney 1-0.

INDIVIDUAL DEFENSIVE STATISTICS

INTERCEPTIONS   LSU — Chevis Jackson 1-0.
TULANE — David Skehan 1-0.

SACKS   LSU — Rahim Alem 1; Al Woods 1.
TULANE — Antonio Harris 2; Adam Kwentua 1; Evan Lee 1; Reggie Scott 1; Justin Adams 0.5; Frank Morton 0.5.

TACKLES   LSU — Craig Steltz 7; Kirston Pittman 7; Darry Beckwith 5; Luke Sanders 4; Rahim Alem 3; Harry Coleman 3; Glenn Dorsey 3.
TULANE — Evan Lee 13; James Dillard 7; Joe Goosby 7; Chinoso Echebelem 6; Josh Lumar 6; David Skehan 6.

ap top 10 released 09.30.07

Wide receiver Chris Mitchell, who had three catches for 32 yards, dives for some extra yards against Tulane.
STAFF PHOTO BY CHRIS GRANGER

1 LSU	2 USC	3 CAL	4 OHIO STATE	5 WISCONSIN	6 SOUTH FLORIDA	7 BOSTON COLLEGE	8 KENTUCKY	9 FLORIDA	10 OKLAHOMA
First-place votes: 33	First-place votes: 32								

florida

LSU safety Craig Steltz goes airborne to tackle
Florida running back Brandon James in the first half.
STAFF PHOTO BY CHRIS GRANGER

TIGERS 28
GATORS 24

10.06.07 | 7:30 p.m. | Tiger Stadium | Baton Rouge, La.

With LSU behind 24-14 in the fourth quarter, Tigers wide receiver Demetrius Byrd hauls in a 4-yard touchdown pass from quarterback Matt Flynn.
STAFF PHOTO BY CHRIS GRANGER

tigers 28
gators 24

BY JAMES VARNEY STAFF WRITER

IN an absolute thriller, No. 1-ranked LSU went for it — literally five times — and came from behind in the fourth quarter to knock off defending national champion Florida 28-24 in Baton Rouge.

The Tigers' five fourth-down conversions, two of which went for touchdowns, were the most glaring difference in a game in which No. 9 Florida (4-2, 0-2 Southeastern Conference) led until 1:09 remained, chiefly because of the dazzling play of quarterback Tim Tebow, who in the first half appeared capable of beating LSU (6-0, 3-0) single-handedly.

A few months later at season's end, Tebow would become the first sophomore to win the Heisman Trophy.

But LSU's defense stepped up when it mattered most, forcing two Gators turnovers in the second half and a critical three-and-out punt after the Tigers scored — again on fourth down — to cut their deficit to 24-21. LSU then produced a memorable eight-minute drive, converting another critical fourth down, and scored when senior running back Jacob Hester bulled his way in from the 2-yard line.

The touchdown set off a frenzied celebration among the record crowd of 92,910 at Tiger Stadium.

The game was a riveting match, one in which both teams topped 300 yards in offense — and LSU approached 400. The Tigers had 25 first downs to Florida's 19, and the teams each punted twice. LSU punished Florida on the ground, lugging the ball 52 times for 247 yards.

"I give great credit to our opponents. We played a great football team," LSU Coach Les Miles said. "I'm awfully proud of this team."

Prior to its dominating fourth quarter, though, it looked

tigers 28 | gators 24

as if LSU, which shot itself in the foot repeatedly and missed two field-goal attempts, might fall short and squander three huge second-half injections of momentum.

The first of those came after the Tigers scored their second touchdown on a 4-yard run by sophomore running back Keiland Williams that pulled LSU to 17-14. That score was made possible by an LSU fake field-goal attempt, this time one that senior quarterback Matt Flynn, the holder, picked up and ran around the right side for a first down.

Seconds later, news broke that No. 2 Southern California had lost to visiting Stanford, a 41-point underdog, 24-23.

Pandemonium reigned. The defeat meant LSU — with a victory — would be poised to be ranked No. 1 the next day.

Certainly Florida, which beat LSU last season in Gainesville en route to its national championship, wasn't about to surrender the mantle of the SEC's best team easily. In the midst of a gyrating, hostile stadium, Tebow led a 75-yard drive that took five plays and less than 2:30. Once again, LSU faced a deficit, this time 10 points — 24-14.

The other jolts for LSU came on turnovers.

Senior linebacker Ali Highsmith forced a fumble on the next to last play of the third quarter, and junior linebacker Darry Beckwith fell on the ball at midfield. But LSU's drive stalled, and junior Colt David missed a 37-yard field-goal attempt wide left — his second miss against the Gators.

On the Gators next possession, however, Tebow's pass was intercepted by senior defensive end Kirston Pittman.

Flashing his gambling instincts, Miles decided to go for it on fourth-and-goal. His gamble paid off when Flynn scrambled to his right, then connected with junior wide receiver Demetrius Byrd in the end zone.

The touchdown cut LSU's deficit to 24-21 and set the stage for a tension-packed final 10 minutes, with Hester eventually scoring from the 2-yard line.

TEAM	1ST	2ND	3RD	4TH	FINAL
Florida	3	14	7	0	24
LSU	0	7	7	14	28

Attendance 92,910 at Tiger Stadium

SCORING SUMMARY

FLORIDA	Joey Ijjas 31-yard field goal. Ten plays, 47 yards in 3:41.
FLORIDA	Kesthan Moore 2-yard pass from TimTebow (Ijjas kick). Twelve 12 plays, 77 yards in 7:03.
LSU	Ryan Perrilloux 1-yard run (Colt David kick). Sixteen plays, 80 yards in 7:37.
FLORIDA	Tebow 9-yard run (Ijjas kick). Ten plays, 72 yards in 3:43.
LSU	Keiland Williams 4-yard run (David kick). Fifteen plays, 70 yards in 7:03.
FLORIDA	Cornelius Ingram 37-yard pass from Tebow (Ijjas kick). Five plays, 75 yards in 2:27.
LSU	Demetrius Byrd 4-yard pass from Matt Flynn (David kick). Five plays, 27 yards in 1:50.
LSU	Jacob Hester 2-yard run (David kick). Fifteen plays, 60 yards in 8:11.

TEAM STATISTICS

TEAM STATISTICS	LSU	FLORIDA
FIRST DOWNS	25	19
RUSHES-YARDS (NET)	52-247	32-156
PASSING YARDS (NET)	144	158
PASSES (ATT-COMP-INT)	28-14-1	26-12-1
TOTAL OFFENSE (PLAYS-YARDS)	80-391	58-314
PENALTIES (NUMBER-YARDS)	7-61	2-8
PUNTS (NUMBER-AVERAGE)	2-49.0	2-37.0
PUNT RETURNS (NUMBER-YARDS-TD)	0-0-0	1-17-0
KICKOFF RETURNS (NUMBER-YARDS-TD)	4-89-0	3-24-0
POSSESSION TIME	35:52	24:08
SACKS BY (YARDS LOST)	2-8	0-0
FIELD GOALS (ATTEMPTED-MADE)	2-0	1-1
FUMBLES-LOST	0-0	2-1

INDIVIDUAL OFFENSIVE STATISTICS

RUSHING LSU — Jacob Hester 23-106; Keiland Williams 9-46; Trindon Holliday 6-33; Matt Flynn 4-30; Ryan Perrilloux 6-23; Charles Scott 4-9. FLORIDA — Kestahn Moore 12-79; Tim Tebow 16-67; Percy Harvin 3-11.

PASSING LSU — Matt Flynn 27/14-1-1, 144; Ryan Perrilloux 1/0-0-0, 0. FLORIDA — Tim Tebow 26/12-2-1, 158.

RECEIVING LSU — Brandon LaFell 6-73; Demetrius Byrd 3-20; Jared Mitchell 2-30; Richard Dickson 1-14; Charles Scott 1-6; Keiland Williams 1-1. FLORIDA — Percy Harvin 4-58; Louis Murphy 3-26; Cornelius Ingram 2-43; Kestahn Moore 2-21; Andre Caldwell 1-10

INDIVIDUAL DEFENSIVE STATISTICS

INTERCEPTIONS LSU — Kirston Pittman 1. FLORIDA — Joe Haden 1.

SACKS LSU — Glenn Dorsey 1; Kirston Pittman 1.

TACKLES LSU — Craig Steltz 16; Curtis Taylor 8; Kirston Pittman 7; Glenn Dorsey 5; Chevis Jackson 5. FLORIDA — Jermaine Cunningham 17; Branson Spikes 11; Major Wright 11; Joe Haden 10; Dustin Doe 9.

ap top 10
released 10.07.07

Quarterback Ryan Perrilloux punctuates a 16-play, 80-yard drive with a 1-yard touchdown run.
STAFF PHOTO BY CHRIS GRANGER

| 1 LSU First-place votes: 65 | 2 CAL | 3 OHIO STATE | 4 BOSTON COLLEGE | 5 SOUTH FLORIDA | 6 OKLAHOMA | 7 SOUTH CAROLINA | 8 WEST VIRGINIA | 9 OREGON | 10 USC |

With Florida leading 24-21 late in the fourth quarter, LSU is determined to score, and Jacob Hester, who finished with 106 yards on 23 carries, does just that on a 2-yard plunge.
STAFF PHOTO BY CHUCK COOK

tigers 28 gators 24

Jacob Hester carries the Tigers on his back

PETER FINNEY

In the end, it was Jacob Hester, legs pumping, body inches from the ground, grunting, groaning his way into the end zone.

It was only a 2-yard run up the gut, but it was the biggest 2 yards of the night for the now unanimous No. 1 LSU Tigers (6-0).

Hester stole the game, not from the Florida Gators, but from their quarterback, Tim Tebow.

Hester stole it like some blue-collar thoroughbred, lighting the fire under the 60-yard drive when all seemed lost, carrying his team to an unforgettable 28-24 victory in Baton Rouge.

This was Tebow's night all right, but Hester simply reached in and grabbed it by the throat with a majestic march that saw the running back out of Shreveport's Evangel High School convert two fourth-and-2's by inches, one from midfield, the other at point-blank range.

All Tebow could do was watch from the sideline, watch Hester get the payoff parade started with a 7-yard slice up the middle, then add a bull rush of 19, then watch LSU, faced with a second-and-18, keep the chains moving by keeping its poise and handing the football to Hester for 4 yards, 2 yards and 3 yards.

And, finally, the final 2 yards that left Hester dizzy, seemingly in a daze after he punched it in with 69 seconds remaining, which, fortunately, was not enough time to allow Florida's virtuoso quarterback to produce one more miracle.

On this night, it was Tebow's heroics that kept a Tiger Stadium crowd in somewhat of a sullen trance. The Gators' quarterback/fullback had a hand in every inch of the 314 yards his team gained, 156 rushing, 158 passing, against a defense kept on its heels.

It was Tebow who opened daylight for everything, and everyone, because the defense had to account for him running the ball or throwing it. He did both with a cunning quickness, speed to the outside, and moxie.

It was the kind of victory LSU Coach Les Miles credited, more than anything, to the "character" of his team.

"We looked defeat in the face and found a way to pull it out against a great football team," he said.

And his team did it less than an hour after Southern California was upset by Stanford, a turn of events that vaulted LSU to No. 1 in all the polls, not simply The Associated Press.

to keep the chains moving, throwing 27 yards to Harvin to put the ball at LSU's 2, ending the drive by going left, then shoveling a 2-yard pass to his halfback on third down.

All along, Tebow had LSU's defense at his mercy.

The Tigers' offense came to life with an 80-yard march Hester got going with his legs, that Flynn kept going with a couple of completions, that sophomore Ryan Perrilloux closed with a quarterback keeper from Florida's 1 on the 16th play to cut LSU's deficit to 10-7.

Jacob Hester stole [the game] like some blue-collar thoroughbred, lighting the fire under the 60-yard drive when all seemed lost, carrying his team to an unforgettable 28-24 victory in Baton Rouge.

"Those two turnovers we had killed us, but you have to give LSU credit," Tebow said. "I like the way Coach Miles went for it on fourth down. He's a gambler just like Coach (Urban) Meyer. He's out there to win."

It didn't take long for Tebow to introduce himself to the No. 1 defense in college football. He started by doing it throwing, not running, throwing to receivers cutting across the middle on slants, before converting a third-and-2 with an 8-yard rush, then becoming a decoy for junior running back Kestahn Moore, who carried for another 15 yards.

Before you knew it, the Gators had a 3-0 lead, thanks to a big defensive play by senior linebacker Ali Highsmith, a deflection of a Tebow fastball to sophomore wide receiver Percy Harvin on third down.

After sophomore wide receiver Brandon LaFell poured cold water on what looked like a promising Tigers drive by dropping a Matt Flynn pass down the middle at the Tigers' 39-yard line that could have gone for long yardage, Tebow was at it again.

This time he marched the Gators 77 yards in 12 plays, drawing attention as he handed off for enough real estate

The home crowd was on its feet, but not for long.

Tebow came on one more time, doing his thing, first with a 19-yard completion, then by propelling his 235 pounds forward for 5 yards, 6 yards, 6 yards and 9 yards, all mixed in with a 15-yard roughing the passer penalty on the Tigers.

Finally, there was Tebow, facing a third-and-goal at LSU's 9, and there was the Tigers' defense, unsure what was coming, then watching the quarterback barrel up the middle to end a march of 72 yards.

Once again, the Gators led by 10, and there it remained at halftime when LSU junior Colt David missed a 43 yard field-goal attempt.

The question was: Would a three-point deficit for the Tigers make a difference on a night that looked like it belonged to one man, a quarterback who also played fullback?

Well, it didn't, that was, until Jacob Hester came along to gain the last of his 106 yards.

Especially the last two.

Cornerback Jonathan Zenon and the fans rejoice after the Tigers held off a last-ditch effort by the Gators.
STAFF PHOTO BY CHUCK COOK

kentucky

In the third overtime and facing fourth and 2, running back Charles Scott comes up 1-yard short against the Wildcats.
STAFF PHOTO BY CHUCK COOK

WILDCATS 43
TIGERS 37 3OT

10.13.07 | 2:30 p.m. | Commonwealth Stadium | Lexington, Ky.

Running back Charles Scott (32) isn't able to hide his emotions as he and offensive lineman Joseph Barksdale exit the field following LSU's loss to Kentucky in triple overtime.
STAFF PHOTO BY CHUCK COOK

wildcats 43
tigers 37

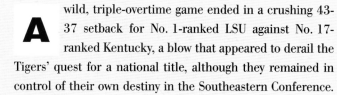

BY JAMES VARNEY STAFF WRITER

A wild, triple-overtime game ended in a crushing 43-37 setback for No. 1-ranked LSU against No. 17-ranked Kentucky, a blow that appeared to derail the Tigers' quest for a national title, although they remained in control of their own destiny in the Southeastern Conference.

Kentucky (6-1, 2-1 SEC) refused to crumple early in the second half when it looked as if LSU had seized control. Instead, the Wildcats started a furious rally from 13 points down that ended with senior quarterback André Woodson throwing for three touchdowns and running for a fourth. Despite the fact that LSU (6-1, 3-1) entered the game in Lexington, Ky., with the nation's best defense, the Wildcats scored on their last six possessions.

The Tigers' vaunted front four never put serious pressure on Woodson, and he repeatedly beat LSU with long and short passes to pick up first downs.

Kentucky also reaped enormous benefits from penalties, including a pass-interference call that went against the Tigers in the fourth quarter, which sustained a Wildcats' scoring drive. LSU, which entered the game as the second most penalized team in the SEC, was flagged 12 times — including two in overtime — for 103 yards. That included a holding call in the end zone after Woodson had thrown an incomplete pass on a third-and-goal from the 6-yard line.

Kentucky was penalized seven times for 62 yards, but LSU Coach Les Miles blamed himself for the loss and did not criticize his players.

"Hell no," he said. "It was kids playing hard. I'm going to tell you right now, I thought this team came here to play, and if anyone wants to challenge me on that, then they have to

| Game 7 | 10.13.07 | Commonwealth Stadium |

wildcats 43 | tigers 37

check the effort, because I looked at it — and I watched it.

"As a coach, I can coach better, and I will. I promise you."

LSU also hurt itself with a myriad of dropped passes, a shortcoming that has plagued the Tigers all season. With the game on the line, the Tigers opted to run the ball instead of pass.

With LSU trailing 43-37 in triple-overtime and facing fourth-and-2 from the 17-yard line, junior linebacker Braxton Kelley plugged a gap and stopped sophomore running back Charles Scott at the 16-yard line.

"He came out of nowhere," Scott said.

Said Tigers senior running back Jacob Hester: "There's no rhyme or reason to it. Kentucky played great, and we got beat. . . . I'm sure Florida felt this same way last week."

As was Tiger Stadium last week in LSU's 28-24 comeback win over the Gators, Commonwealth Stadium was overflowing with euphoria. Many of the 70,902 in attendance — Kentucky's fourth-largest home crowd — spilled onto the turf after the school's first win over a No. 1-ranked team since 1964. The victory also avenged the Wildcats' 49-0 loss to the Tigers last year in Baton Rouge.

"I'm so very, very proud of these young men," Kentucky Coach Rich Brooks said. "The guts and the backbone and the character to keep coming back when things didn't look good, particularly in the third quarter when they came out and went up by 13."

The three overtimes — the first multiple-overtime game LSU had played — began with Kentucky freshman third-string tailback Derrick Locke scoring on a 1-yard run. LSU answered with a 2-yard misdirection pitch to redshirt fresh-

man running back Richard Murphy for a touchdown.

In the second overtime, each team kicked a field goal, sending it to triple overtime tied at 37.

Aided by a holding call against junior safety Curtis Taylor, Woodson connected with senior Steve Johnson for a 7-yard touchdown pass in the third overtime. Senior cornerback Jonathan Zenon, victimized all game by Kentucky, collided with Johnson on the play and lay sprawled on the goal line.

The two-point conversion attempt for the Wildcats failed, giving the Tigers renewed hope.

On three consecutive plays, LSU gave the ball to Hester, but he was able to muster just 8 yards on the ground. After calling a timeout, Scott was stopped short on fourth down.

"We've got a team that's sick," Miles said. "I did not enjoy this. We're going to have to regroup, going to have to work hard and get ready for another game next week."

TEAM	1ST	2ND	3RD	4TH	1OT	2OT	3OT	FINAL
LSU	0	17	10	0	7	3	0	37
Kentucky	7	7	7	6	7	3	6	43

Attendance 70,902 at Commonwealth Stadium

TEAM STATISTICS	LSU	KENTUCKY
FIRST DOWNS	22	24
RUSHES-YARDS	50-261	41-125
PASSING YARDS (NET)	142	250
PASSES (ATT-COMP-INT)	37-18-1	38-21-2
TOTAL OFFENSE (PLAYS-YARDS)	87-403	79-375
PENALTIES (NUMBER-YARDS)	12-103	7-62
PUNTS (NUMBER-AVERAGE)	4-33.8	3-47.3
PUNT RETURNS (NUMBER-YARDS-TD)	0-0-0	1-1-0
KICKOFF RETURNS (NUMBER-YARDS-TD)	3-86-0	6-140-0
POSSESSION TIME	33:21	26:39
SACKS BY (YARDS LOST)	0-0	3-15
FIELD GOALS (ATTEMPTED-MADE)	4-3	3-3
FUMBLES-LOST	0-0	3-0

ap top 10

released 10.14.07

| 1 OHIO STATE Avg.: .9416 | 2 SOUTH FLORIDA .9200 | 3 BOSTON COLLEGE .8906 | 4 LSU .8400 | 5 OKLAHOMA .7623 | 6 SOUTH CAROLINA .7432 | 7 KENTUCKY .7432 | 8 ARIZONA STATE .6831 | 9 WEST VIRGINIA .6624 | 10 OREGON .6369 |

Tigers running back Jacob Hester draws a crowd against the Wildcats.
STAFF PHOTO BY CHUCK COOK

SCORING SUMMARY

UK	T.C. Drake 2-yard pass from André Woodson (Lones Seiber kick). Twelve plays, 49 yards in 4:53.
LSU	Charles Scott 1-yard run (Colt David kick). Eight plays, 79 yards in 2:54.
LSU	Colt David 31-yard field goal. Twelve plays, 68 yards in 5:42.
LSU	Scott 13-yard run (David kick). Eight plays, 46 yards in 3:37.
UK	Woodson 12-yard run (Seiber kick). Five plays, 78 yards in 0:37.
LSU	Richard Dickson 4-yard pass from Matt Flynn (David kick). Eleven plays, 52 yards in 5:39.
LSU	David 30-yard field goal. Eleven plays, 38 yards in 4:19.
UK	Jacob Tamme 8-yard pass from Woodson (Seiber kick). Seven plays, 82 yards in 2:30.
UK	Seiber 33-yard field goal. Thirteen plays, 48 yards in 6:54.
UK	Seiber 27-yard field goal. Seven plays, 53 yards in 2:47.
UK	Derrick Locke 1-yard run (Seiber kick). Five plays, 25 yards.
LSU	Richard Murphy 2-yard run (David kick). Four plays, 25 yards.
LSU	David 38-yard field goal. Four plays, 4 yards.
UK	Seiber 43-yard field goal. Four plays, 0 yards.
UK	Steve Johnson 7-yard pass from Woodson (two-point conversion attempt failed). Eight plays, 25 yards.

INDIVIDUAL OFFENSIVE STATISTICS

RUSHING   LSU — Charles Scott 7-94; Jacob Hester 18-61; Matt Flynn 10-53; Trindon Holliday 5-24; Ryan Perrilloux 5-15; Richard Murphy 3-10; Keiland Williams 1-5; Terrance Toliver 1 minus-1.

KENTUCKY — Derrick Locke 20-64; Tony Dixon 17-45; André Woodson 3-16.

PASSING   LSU — Matt Flynn 35/17-1-1, 130; Ryan Perrilloux 2/1-0-0, 12.

KENTUCKY — André Woodson 38/21-3-2, 250.

RECEIVING   LSU — Brandon LaFell 4-42; Richard Dickson 4-33; Richard Murphy 2-22; Jared Mitchell 2-9; Charles Scott 2-6; Demetrius Byrd 1-13; Chris Mitchell 1-8; Keiland Williams 1-5; Jacob Hester 1-4.

KENTUCKY — Steve Johnson 7-134; Dicky Lyons 6-49; Jacob Tamme 3-33; Keenan Burton 2-13; Tony Dixon 1-18; T.C. Drake 1-2; Maurice Grinter 1-1.

INDIVIDUAL DEFENSIVE STATISTICS

INTERCEPTIONS   LSU — Chevis Jackson 1; Chad Jones 1.

KENTUCKY — Trevard Lindley 1.

SACKS   KENTUCKY — Ventrell Jenkins 2; Dominic Lewis 1.

TACKLES   LSU — Darry Beckwith 12; Ali Highsmith 8; Tyson Jackson 8; Craig Steltz 8; Kirston Pittman 7; Danny McCray 6; Jonathan Zenon 6.

KENTUCKY — Wesley Woodyard 11; Jeremy Jarmon 10; Ashton Cobb 7; Trevard Lindley 7; Paul Warford 7.

| 1 OHIO STATE First-place votes: 50 | 2 SOUTH FLORIDA First-place votes: 11 | 3 BOSTON COLLEGE First place votes: 1 | 4 OKLAHOMA | 5 LSU | 6 SOUTH CAROLINA | 7 OREGON | 8 KENTUCKY | 9 WEST VIRGINIA | 10 CAL |

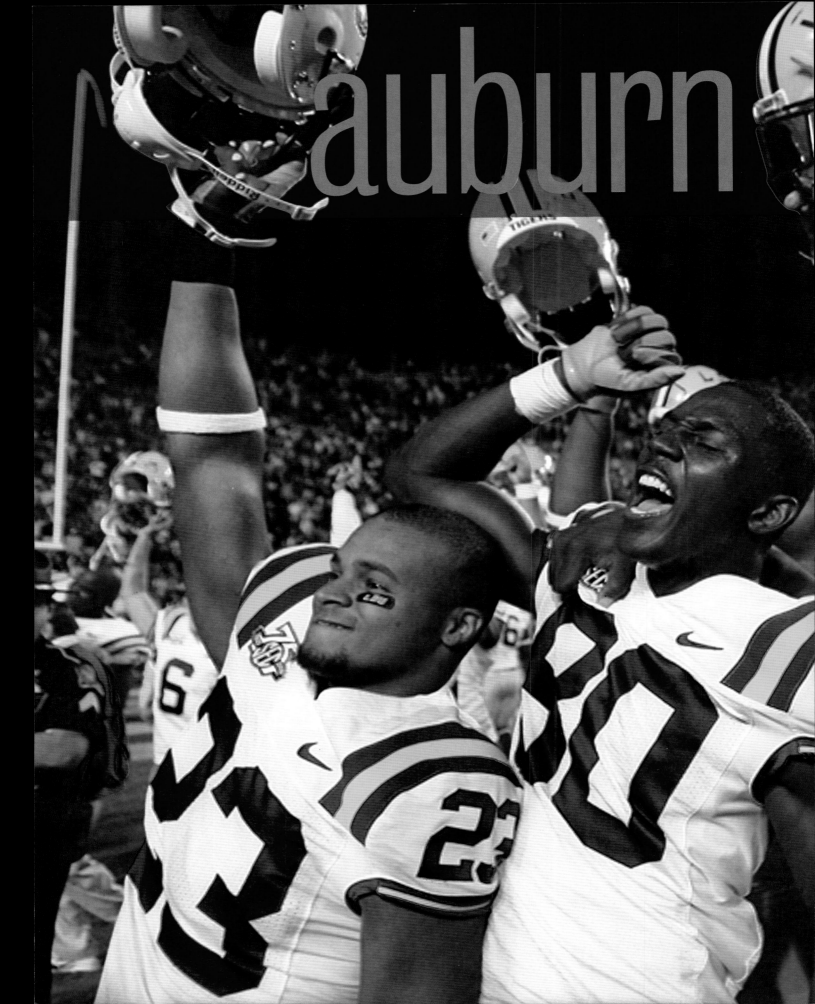

auburn

LSU | 30
AUBURN | 24

10.20.07 | 8 p.m. | Tiger Stadium | Baton Rouge, La.

Coach Les Miles, players and the staff let out a roar near the student section at Tiger Stadium after LSU scored 17 points in the fourth quarter to rally past Auburn.
STAFF PHOTO BY JOHN McCUSKER

lsu 30
auburn 24

BY JAMES VARNEY STAFF WRITER

Quarterback Ryan Perrilloux is determined to get upfield, but Auburn linebacker Bo Harris presents a formidable challenge.
STAFF PHOTO BY JOHN McCUSKER

There's no such thing as dull with LSU. In its third unbearably tense game in a row, fifth-year senior quarterback Matt Flynn connected with junior wide receiver Demetrius Byrd on a 22-yard touchdown pass with one second remaining to lift LSU to a 30-24 victory over Auburn in Baton Rouge.

With the win, LSU (7-1, 4-1 Southeastern Conference) kept alive its hopes of a national title and, equally important, sat in command of the SEC Western Division.

For No. 8 Auburn (5-3, 3-2), the loss was excruciating, especially after it had taken a 24-23 lead with barely three minutes remaining. Auburn marched 83 yards in nine plays to retake the lead in the fourth quarter after LSU had scored 16 consecutive second-half points.

A short kickoff, though, gave LSU — needing only a field goal to win — possession of the ball on its 48-yard line.

LSU maneuvered the ball to Auburn's 22-yard line in the waning moments, appearing to get into position to set up for a field-goal attempt for the victory.

Instead, on third down, LSU Coach Les Miles elected to take a shot at the end zone, and the gamble paid off big when Byrd ducked under his coverage and hauled in Flynn's pass. Byrd tumbled into the left corner of the end zone, then stood exultant before the student section holding the ball aloft.

The LSU sideline was spellbound for a faction of a second, then delirious as the referees signaled touchdown.

The game was a typical Auburn-LSU affair, in that the previous three contests were decided by a total of eight points. LSU's win also continued a streak of eight games in which the home team had won.

| Game 8 | 10.20.07 | Tiger Stadium |

lsu 30 auburn 24

Still, it looked as if Auburn, which had played superbly on the road in SEC games in recent weeks, would steal one on hostile turf. Although the Flynn-to-Byrd connection was the moment to remember, perhaps the true difference was senior wide receiver Early Doucet.

Doucet, who was sidelined for more than a month with an injury that LSU never divulged, returned to the lineup against Auburn, and his presence gave the team a desperately needed spark.

Doucet finished with seven catches for 93 yards.

But the shortcomings that have plagued LSU this season were glaring once again: in particular, the failure of the team's wide receivers to catch the ball. Sophomore wide receiver Brandon LaFell, who had dropped multiple passes in every game he played, turned a long gain into a bobble and an interception in the third quarter, killing a scoring chance.

Similarly, at the end of the first half, Byrd dropped a pass that would have given LSU an opportunity to continue a drive.

Auburn set the tone when it took the opening kickoff and methodically marched steadily down field, converting third downs seemingly at ease. The 63-yard drive was capped when senior quarterback Brandon Cox, scrambling to his left, connected with sophomore wide receiver Montez Billings on a 17-yard touchdown pass.

Sophomore running back Keiland Williams fumbled the ensuing kickoff, and things seemed awry for LSU. But Williams redeemed himself later in the quarter. He took a screen pass in front of LSU's bench, squirted through an opening along the line when he appeared trapped for a short gain, and raced 46 yards to the end zone, tying the score at 7.

But two series later, LSU sophomore backup quarterback Ryan Perrilloux fumbled on an option play. The ball popped into the hands of sophomore cornerback Jerraud Powers, who sprinted toward the end zone but was dragged down from behind by sophomore wide receiver Trindon Holliday at LSU's 3-yard line.

Three plays later, with the ball on the 1-yard line, senior tailback Carl Stewart leapt into the end zone to give Auburn a 14-7 lead.

With 12:55 remaining, LSU senior running back Jacob Hester stretched across the goal line on a 5-yard pass, capping an eight-play, 85-yard drive. The score put LSU ahead for the first time, 20-17.

Unfazed, Cox moved Auburn back down the field. And when he connected with junior wide receiver Rodgeriqus Smith on a 3-yard touchdown pass to give Auburn a 24-23 lead, it seemed this Tiger Stadium thriller would go against LSU.

TEAM	1ST	2ND	3RD	4TH	FINAL
Auburn	7	10	0	7	24
LSU	7	0	6	17	30
Attendance				92,630 at Tiger Stadium	

SCORING SUMMARY

AUBURN Montez Billings 17-yard pass from Brandon Cox (Wes Byrum kick). Eleven plays, 63 yards in 4:50.

LSU Keiland Williams 46-yard pass from Matt Flynn (Colt David kick). Four plays, 62 yards in 1:46.

AUBURN Carl Stewart 1-yard run (Byrum kick). Three plays, 3 yards in 1:23.

AUBURN Byrum 22-yard field goal. Twelve plays, 90 yards in 5:12.

LSU David 29-yard field goal. Eight plays, 56 yards in 3:39.

LSU David 26-yard field goal. Five plays, 58 yards in 0:53.

LSU Jacob Hester 5-yard pass from Flynn (David kick). Eight plays, 85 yards in 2:18.

LSU David 33-yard field goal. Seven plays, 55 yards in 2:54.

AUBURN Rodgeriqus Smith 3-yard pass from Cox (Byrum kick). Nine plays, 83 yards in 4:43.

LSU Demetrius Byrd 22-yard pass from Flynn (David kick). Nine plays, 58 yards in 3:12.

Running back Keiland Williams scores on a 46-yard strike from Matt Flynn against Auburn in the first quarter.

STAFF PHOTO BY JOHN McCUSKER

TEAM STATISTICS	LSU	AUBURN
FIRST DOWNS	23	16
RUSHES-YARDS	33-169	35-97
PASSING YARDS	319	199
PASSES (ATT-COMP-INT)	35-22-1	28-18-0
TOTAL OFFENSE (PLAYS-YARDS)	68-488	63-296
PENALTIES (NUMBER-YARDS)	5-35	3-20
PUNTS (NUMBER-AVERAGE)	4-52.0	7-43.1
PUNT RETURNS (NUMBER-YARDS-TD)	4-35-0	0-0-0
KICKOFF RETURNS (NUMBER-YARDS-TD)	3-6-0	7-135-0
POSSESSION TIME	27:16	32:44
SACKS BY (YARDS LOST)	2-9	2-18
FIELD GOALS (ATTEMPTED-MADE)	3-3	1-1
FUMBLES-LOST	3-1	0-0

INDIVIDUAL OFFENSIVE STATISTICS

RUSHING LSU — Jacob Hester 9-50; Matt Flynn 10-34; Charles Scott 5-28; Trindon Holliday 1-17; Terrance Toliver 1-17; Ryan Perrilloux 4-11.
AUBURN — Brad Lester 16-68; Ben Tate 10-17; Brandon Cox 6-12; Carl Stewart 1-1; Kodi Burns 1-1.

PASSING LSU — Matt Flynn 34/22-3-1, 319; Ryan Perrilloux 1/0-0-0, 0.
AUBURN — Brandon Cox 28/18-2-0, 199.

RECEIVING LSU — Early Doucet 7-93; Demetrius Byrd 3-89; Richard Dickson 3-31; Brandon LaFell 3-18; Terrance Toliver 2-19; Jacob Hester 2-6.
AUBURN — Montez Billings 6-78; Rodgerious Smith 6-56; Brad Lester 5-56.

INDIVIDUAL DEFENSIVE STATISTICS

INTERCEPTIONS AUBURN — Patrick Lee 1.
SACKS LSU — Ali Highsmith 1; Tremaine Johnson 1.
AUBURN — Quentin Groves 1, Sen'Derrick Marks 1.
TACKLES LSU — Ali Highsmith 11; Craig Steltz 10; Chevis Jackson 7; Darry Beckwith 6; Marlon Favorite 6; Glenn Dorsey 5; Curtis Taylor 5.
AUBURN — Eric Brock 11; Josh Thompson 10; Chris Evans 7; Zac Etheridge 6; Jerraud Powers 6.

1 OHIO STATE First-place votes: 57	2 BOSTON COLLEGE First-place votes: 2	3 LSU First-place votes: 5	4 OKLAHOMA	5 OREGON	6 WEST VIRGINIA	7 ARIZONA STATE First-place votes: 1	8 VIRGINIA TECH	9 FLORIDA	10 USC

lsu's 2007 championship season 57

Early Doucet returns with a bang from a five-game absence due to an unspecified injury. The wide receiver had seven catches for 93 yards.

STAFF PHOTO BY JOHN McCUSKER

lsu 30 | auburn 24

Doucet looms large in return for LSU

JOHN DeSHAZIER

From afar, all it looked like senior wide receiver Early Doucet did against Auburn was save LSU's season.

All he did was step into the mix against a formidable opponent after an undisclosed injury led to a five-game absence, catch just about everything within his reach and inspire a team that appeared gazing into the abyss, one that appeared to be looking for a way to hand over a game it couldn't afford to drop if it hoped to continue progressing toward a division, conference and national title.

And if you knew anything about LSU's receiving woes during Doucet's forced break, you knew how much his presence meant during LSU's 30-24 victory in Baton Rouge.

LSU's receivers consistently had difficulty catching passes with or without Doucet in the lineup. They were not young men you'd want handling newborns or eggs, based on the frequency they've dropped catchable passes week after week after week.

After yet another costly no-hands job by sophomore receiver Brandon LaFell against Auburn, in which the ball was tipped into the hands of defensive back Patrick Lee at Auburn's 14-yard line in the third quarter, LaFell mercifully was benched.

Quarterback Matt Flynn simply couldn't continue to have faith in a receiving corps that was as likely, or more likely, to drop a perfectly thrown pass as it was to catch it.

He did want to throw to Doucet, though.

And he did, seven times for 93 yards against Auburn.

Sure, Demetrius Byrd caught the game-winner — a 22-yard strike with a second left — to cap LSU's second consecutive, breathtaking, heart-pounding, come-from-behind victory at Tiger Stadium.

But neither Byrd nor anyone else was in position to do much of anything heroic if not for a 33-yard catch by Doucet on a third-and-9 on the opening possession of the third quarter, the one that lifted a team that was running low on fuel and time.

LSU's Demetrius Byrd has his hands full against Auburn safety Eric Brock in the first half

STAFF PHOTO BY JOHN McCUSKER

lsu 30   auburn 24

That catch led to a field goal that cut Auburn's lead to 17-10, awakened a somber LSU crowd, infused a lifeless offense and, most important, showed that Doucet was back in a big way.

He caught two more passes, for 26 yards, on LSU's next possession, was Flynn's target on a couple of incompletions on the next drive, and displayed sure hands a few times in the fourth quarter, too.

But, again, the numbers couldn't possibly measure up to his importance, couldn't possibly measure up to his presence.

LSU needed every bit of it to avoid another fall.

True, it makes for great theater and greater storytelling, this recently developed habit of trying to come from behind and pull out games at the very end.

But the truth is it's a dangerous way to go about handling business — a really, really dangerous way.

Sure, Demetrius Byrd caught the game-winner ... But neither Byrd nor anyone else was in position to do much of anything heroic if not for a 33-yard catch by Doucet on a third-and-9 in the third quarter, the one that lifted a team that was running low on fuel and time.

That's not to say a team can't accomplish each and every one of those goals in such a manner, because LSU, skittish and loose the past two weeks, remains on path to do just that after taking down Auburn.

But it's not a very nerve-calming way of doing things.

Not after a 43-37, triple overtime loss to Kentucky, which doesn't look like an aberration and showed that, perhaps, LSU might not quite be what we thought it was in terms of a dominant force that would go undefeated and drill holes through opponents.

And not after beating Auburn in as gutsy a manner as could be scripted, with a touchdown on the last offensive play.

What was calming was the return of Early, though. And it'll continue to be.

alabama

With the score tied at 3, LSU cornerback Chevis Jackson intercepts Alabama quarterback John Parker Wilson and then takes the high road to the Crimson Tide's 12-yard line.
STAFF PHOTO BY CHRIS GRANGER

TIGERS | 41
CRIMSON TIDE | 34

11.03.07 | 4 p.m. | Bryant-Denny Stadium | Tuscaloosa, Ala.

In a highly anticipated matchup that didn't disappoint, the coaches — LSU's Les Miles and Alabama's Nick Saban — exchange pleasantries following the Tigers' dramatic victory. Saban coached LSU to the national title during the 2003 season. **AP PHOTO/WIDE WORLD PHOTOS**

tigers 41
crimson tide 34

BY JAMES VARNEY STAFF WRITER

They say that every game matters, but the true fan knows that's only half right. Some matter more than others.

Teetering on the brink of self-destruction, the Tigers (8-1, 5-1 Southeastern Conference) somehow summoned an inspired burst against No. 17 Alabama (6-3, 4-2) and scored 17 points in the fourth quarter to snatch a miraculous 41-34 victory in Tuscaloosa, Ala.

In a saner season, the win would have allowed Tigers fans to focus on their team's commanding position atop the SEC Western Division and savor the fact that a shot at a national championship remained viable.

But this has not been that season, and this was not that game. The much heralded matchup between LSU Coach Les Miles and the man he replaced in Baton Rouge, Alabama Coach Nick Saban, lived up to its sky-high pregame hype.

Though both coaches insisted the game had everything to do with championship aspirations and nothing to do with the sideline brain trust, Miles nevertheless got the win the LSU faithful thirsted for more than any other.

It followed the same dramatic script LSU has used for four games.

Trailing 34-27 after Crimson Tide sophomore defensive back Javier Arenas returned a punt 61 yards and threw most of the 92,138 at Bryant-Denny Stadium into delirium, fifth-year senior quarterback Matt Flynn stepped up. He led LSU on an 84-yard march, culminating with a 32-yard touchdown pass to senior wide receiver Early Doucet.

Facing fourth and 4, Flynn connected with Doucet, who, shedding one tackler and juking another, sprinted to the

tigers 41 | crimson tide 34

end zone with his second touchdown catch against the Tide.

Then, just when it appeared the game was headed to overtime, LSU's defense came up with a huge play.

Freshman cornerback Chad Jones stormed up the middle untouched on a third-down play and stripped junior quarterback John Parker Wilson of the ball. It bounded toward Alabama's end zone, and junior safety Curtis Taylor corralled it at the 3-yard line.

Senior Jacob Hester needed two bulldog runs, vaulting over the pile on the second, to score on a 1-yard run to give the Tigers the lead for good.

Despite the thrilling comeback, Miles wasn't about to throw his players any bouquets.

In truth, it was a game LSU should have won easily were it not for a second-quarter dissolution. So grotesque was the breakdown that Alabama led at halftime, despite statistics that showed it had accomplished little. For example, Alabama had minus-12 yards rushing on 14 carries, and Wilson was sacked three times, completing just five of 18 passes with an interception.

But on those five completions Alabama gained 147 yards and scored two touchdowns. LSU defensive coordinator Bo Pelini said he couldn't recall being in a locker room at halftime in which his defense had so dominated an opponent and yet be losing.

Alabama stayed in the game because LSU could not stop wounding itself. In the end, the Tigers were called for 14 penalties and committed three turnovers.

"That was the ugliest win I have ever seen," Miles said as he left the field. "I can only tell you there's a fighting heart in that room, and I enjoy coaching this team. But they will not enjoy me on Monday."

Clutching a game ball the players awarded him, Miles pronounced it the last gift the players would be in any mood to give him for quite a while.

On the other hand, it wasn't as if every call went against the Tigers.

Three plays were reversed on review, including two that were ruled LSU turnovers on the field. Neither of those were bigger, however, than a 41-yard pass from Wilson to senior

TEAM	1ST	2ND	3RD	4TH	FINAL
LSU	10	7	7	17	41
Alabama	3	17	7	7	34

Attendance 92,138 at Bryant-Denny Stadium

SCORING SUMMARY

ALA — Leigh Tiffin 36-yard field goal. Ten plays, 44 yards in 2:30.

LSU — Colt David 43-yard field goal. Eleven plays, 59 yards in 7:01.

LSU — Early Doucet 10-yard pass from Matt Flynn (David kick). Three plays, 12 yards in 0:59.

LSU — Jacob Hester 1-yard run (David kick). Six plays, 54 yards in 2:19.

ALA — DJ Hall 67-yard pass from John Parker Wilson (Tiffin kick). Four plays, 80 yards in 0:56.

ALA — Tiffin 21-yard field goal. Four plays, 0 yards in 0:54.

ALA — Keith Brown 29-yard pass from Wilson (Tiffin kick). Two plays, 20 yards in 0:21.

ALA — Brown 14-yard pass from Wilson (Tiffin kick). Eight plays, 80 yards in 3:07.

LSU — Demetrius Byrd 61-yard pass from Flynn (David kick). Two plays, 72 yards in 0:59.

LSU — David 49-yard field goal. Five plays, 42 yards in 2:07.

ALA — Javier Arenas 61-yard punt return (Tiffin kick).

LSU — Early Doucet 32-yard pass from Flynn (David kick). Ten plays, 84 yards in 2:04.

LSU — Hester 1-yard run (David kick). Two plays, 3 yards in 0:13.

TEAM STATISTICS

TEAM STATISTICS	LSU	ALABAMA
FIRST DOWNS	21	20
RUSHES-YARDS (NET)	34-87	33-20
PASSING YARDS (NET)	388	234
PASSES (ATT-COMP-INT)	46-25-3	40-14-1
TOTAL OFFENSE (PLAYS-YARDS)	80-475	73-254
PENALTIES (NUMBER-YARDS)	14-130	2-15
PUNTS (NUMBER-AVERAGE)	6-46.0	8-33.4
PUNT RETURNS (NUMBER-YARDS-TD)	3-18-0	3-69-1
KICKOFF RETURNS (NUMBER-YARDS-TD)	7-106-0	8-168-0
POSSESSION TIME	33:17	26:43
SACKS BY (YARDS LOST)	7-53	3-19
FIELD GOALS (ATTEMPTED-MADE)	3-2	2-2
FUMBLES-LOST	1-0	2-1

INDIVIDUAL OFFENSIVE STATISTICS

RUSHING — LSU — Jacob Hester 16-47; Keiland Williams 3-24; Matt Flynn 10-19; Trindon Holliday 1-2; Richard Murphy 1-0; Charles Scott 1 minus-1. ALABAMA — Jonathan Lowe 10-31; Terry Grant 13-23; DJ Hall 1-0; John Parker Wilson 9 minus-34.

PASSING — LSU — Matt Flynn 44/24-3-3, 353; Early Doucet 1/1-0-0, 35. ALABAMA — John Parker Wilson 40/14-3-1, 234.

RECEIVING — LSU — Demetrius Byrd 6-61; Early Doucet 5-32; Jacob Hester 5-18; Brandon LaFell 4-19; Richard Dickson 3-35; Matt Flynn 1-35. ALABAMA — Matt Caddell 3-55; Terry Grant 3-29; DJ Hall 2-76; Keith Brown 2-43; Nick Walker 2-25; Mike McCoy 1-4; Jonathan Lowe 1-2.

INDIVIDUAL DEFENSIVE STATISTICS

INTERCEPTIONS — LSU — Chevis Jackson 1. ALABAMA — Kareem Jackson 1; Rashad Johnson 1; Ezekial Knight 1.

SACKS — LSU — Tyson Jackson 2; Chad Jones 2; Kirston Pittman 2; Glenn Dorsey 1. ALABAMA — Wallace Gilberry 3.

TACKLES — LSU — Darry Beckwith 7; Glenn Dorsey 5; Danny McCray 5; Kirston Pittman 5; Chad Jones 4; Craig Steltz 4. ALABAMA — Rashad Johnson 9; Wallace Gilberry 8; Rolando McClain 7; Kareem Jackson 6; Marcus Carter 5; Lorenzo Washington 5.

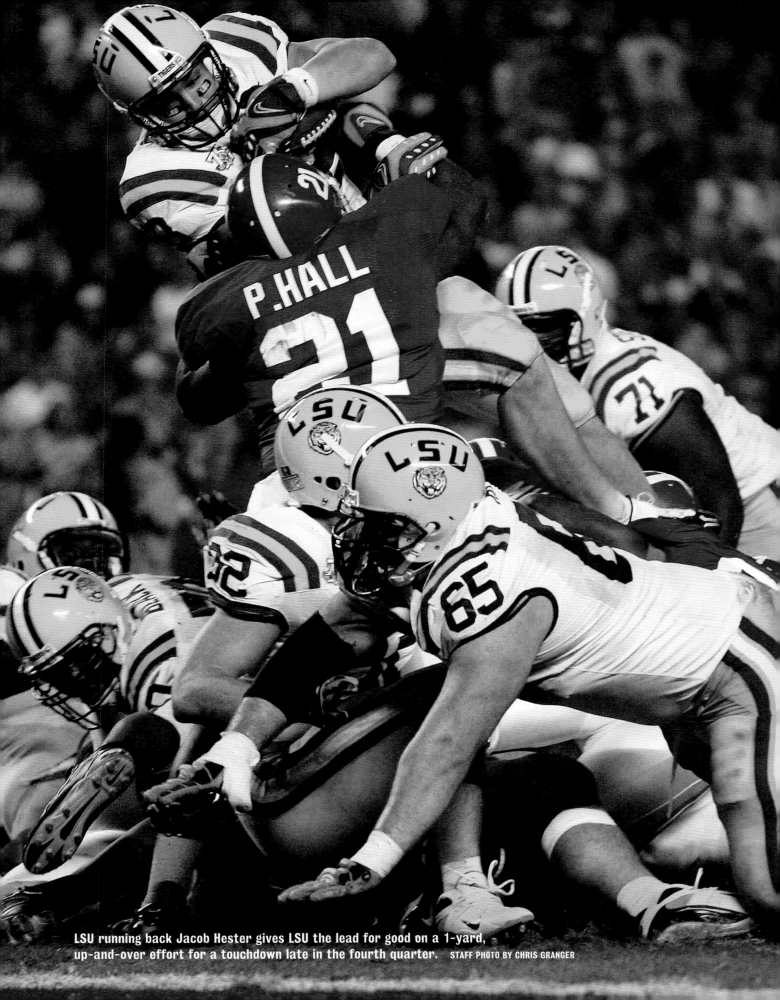

LSU running back Jacob Hester gives LSU the lead for good on a 1-yard, up-and-over effort for a touchdown late in the fourth quarter. STAFF PHOTO BY CHRIS GRANGER

| Game 9 | 11.03.07 | Tiger Stadium |

tigers 41 crimson tide 34

wide receiver Matt Caddell with 11 minutes remaining that would have given Alabama a first down at LSU's 15-yard line.

Instead, the Tide was left with a third-and-19 and was forced to punt.

At the outset, it appeared the Tigers would turn the game into a rout when, after Alabama opened the scoring on a 36-yard field goal by sophomore Leigh Tiffin, LSU responded with 17 unanswered points.

LSU tied the score on Colt David's 43-yard field goal, and, on the next series, senior cornerback Chevis Jackson stepped in front of a Wilson pass at Alabama's 30-yard line and returned it to the 12. Three plays later Flynn hit Doucet on an underneath screen pass that Doucet gathered in near the 6-yard line, sprinted through a seam and tumbled into the end zone.

The second drive featured a reverse flea-flicker in which Hester flipped it to Doucet, who in turn hit Flynn down the right sideline for 35 yards, setting the Tigers up at Alabama's 19. On the first play of the second quarter, Hester plunged over from the 1-yard line to put LSU ahead 17-3.

At that point, however, LSU's fortunes unraveled in a blizzard of yellow flags and ill-advised throws by Flynn. Three interceptions and nine penalties led to 17 consecutive points for Alabama, and the team led 20-17 entering the third quarter.

But Miles said no one panicked at halftime.

"It was like I had to give them enlightenment and let them know we don't have to play that poorly," he said. "I just wanted them to go back out and play the way they intended to play when we came here."

LSU quarterback Matt Flynn dives for extra yardage against Alabama. Flynn gained 19 yards on 10 carries, but he was more effective in the air against the Crimson Tide, throwing three touchdowns.
STAFF PHOTO BY CHRIS GRANGER

With the fourth quarter dwindling down and the score tied at 34, LSU safety Chad Jones sacks John Parker Wilson, who fumbles, opening the door for the Tigers.
STAFF PHOTO BY CHRIS GRANGER

Tigers turn the tables on former coach Saban

PETER FINNEY

The defensive call was "whistle," code name for a five-man blitz that came with Alabama facing a third-and-12 from its 30-yard line.

It triggered LSU's best run of a long night, a mere 12 yards.

That was the distance Chad Jones traveled before making contact with John Parker Wilson, the Alabama quarterback.

In came Jones, the freshman safety, down went a retreating Wilson, and out came the football, finally ending up in the arms of junior safety Curtis Taylor at Alabama's 3-yard line.

Two plays later, with a minute and a half remaining, Jacob Hester was punching it in for the winning points in a spectacular, bizarre 41-34 victory that left the home crowd in Tuscaloosa, Ala., sagging in disbelief.

Later that night, when previously unbeaten Boston College fell 27-17 to Florida State, LSU gained control of its destiny in the national championship picture.

With the sack and fumble, a game that Nick Saban's Crimson Tide appeared to have wrapped up belonged to Les Miles' Tigers, who found a way to overcome 130 yards of penalties and three Matt Flynn interceptions.

How did they do it?

Well, with less than three minutes to go, Early Doucet was stutter-stepping his way to a 32-yard touchdown after catching a Flynn pass over the middle and putting a classic juke on Javier Arenas, the guy who went from hero to goat, first with a 61-yard punt return to put the Tide ahead, then quickly gave it back when Doucet faked him out of his cleats.

"He thought I was going left and I went right," Doucet said. "That's really all it was, one move and I saw the end zone coming up."

The Tigers needed this kind of virtuosity on a night they were left bleeding with 14 flags.

| Game 9 | 11.03.07 | Tiger Stadium |

tigers 41   crimson tide 34

"We made as many mistakes as I've seen any team make," Miles said, "I don't know if I've ever been around a team that played so poorly, making mistake after mistake. We have to improve in this area to be something special. That's our goal."

On this night, the better team, but less-disciplined one, survived when all seemed lost.

"To win like we did," Flynn said, "does one thing as far as I'm concerned. It shows the never-give-up attitude our guys have. I contributed with some bad throws but I always felt, even when we blew a 17-3 lead, that we had the moxie to come back."

Saban agreed.

"They had seven sacks and lots of pressures," he said. "They were lots of times when we didn't have anywhere to throw it, then times when we couldn't make the throw. They have an outstanding team.

"Offensively, in terms of protecting the quarterback, they were able to make the throws to win. We made some big plays, all right, but we didn't have the consistency we needed."

Alabama made enough big plays to keep the Tigers' feet to the fire and keep the home crowd in the game.

At halftime, Bama not only was in the game, but leading, despite negative rushing yards and a quarterback who had completed only five of 18 passes.

"Our defense came up big when it had to," Miles said, "that's the biggest thing. I thought Glenn Dorsey, playing at less than half speed, was outstanding. The guys feed off someone like Glenn. He got nicked early, but there was no way he was going to stay out. He's an unbelievable football player."

How good is LSU?

"I wish I could tell you," Miles said. "We have to play better than we did to accomplish the things we hope to. I can tell you that. I think we know that. We beat a real spunky outfit tonight. But we have to lift our game to keep on going. I think we will."

LSU tight end Mit Cole (81) is jazzed after Colt David (6) made a 49-yard field goal to tie the score at 27 in the fourth quarter.
STAFF PHOTO BY CHRIS GRANGER

la. tech

Running back Jacob Hester, who finished with 115 yards on 11 carries, bolted on an 87-yard touchdown run as the Bulldogs ran out of gas.

STAFF PHOTO BY JOHN McCUSKER

TIGERS 58
BULLDOGS 10
11.10.07 | 7 p.m. | Tiger Stadium | Baton Rouge, La.

tigers 58
bulldogs 10

BY JAMES VARNEY STAFF WRITER

T he 58-10 final score of LSU's victory over Louisiana Tech is misleading. Given the listless aura that overhung the Tigers' homecoming, one would have thought everything had been handed to LSU before the kickoff.

And, in a way, it was.

Although LSU built what would prove an insurmountable 27-7 lead by halftime, the game was a strangely dispirited affair marred by repeated long delays because of clock malfunctions, replay reviews and, at one point, a compound leg fracture suffered by a line judge who was wheeled off on a stretcher.

LSU did jolt the crowd out of its lethargy twice on scoring passes, particularly a 71-yard pass from fifth-year senior Matt Flynn to freshman wide receiver Terrance Toliver, but were it not for a couple of botched snaps by Louisiana Tech, the score might have been closer.

Louisiana Tech fumbled the snap on the second play of the game, and the Tigers recovered on the Bulldogs' 24-yard line. That set up a 1-yard scoring sneak by Flynn less than three minutes into the game.

Though Louisiana Tech moved the ball early, even outgaining LSU and racking up more first downs in the first quarter, its drives invariably stalled inside LSU territory.

The Tigers, on the other hand, also made the least out of some favorable field position. After the Bulldogs' snap on a punt ricocheted off the center's leg, LSU had a first down at Louisiana Tech's 18. But the Tigers could not advance the ball and settled for a 31-yard field goal by junior Colt David.

Running back Keiland Williams and the Tigers proved too much for the Bulldogs. LSU finished with 595 yards on offense.
STAFF PHOTO BY JOHN McCUSKER

| Game 10 | 11.10.07 | Tiger Stadium |

tigers 58   bulldogs 10

The Bulldogs managed a two-play, 52-yard scoring drive capped by a 37-yard pass from senior quarterback Zac Champion to wide receiver Brian Jackson at the beginning of the second quarter. That cut the Bulldogs' deficit to three points, but that was as close as Louisiana Tech could get.

The second half unfolded before a thinning crowd and yet showcased some of the most explosive football of the evening. David stretched LSU's lead to 30-7 with a 28-yard field goal on the opening drive, and then the Bulldogs unraveled.

Tailback Jacob Hester squirted through a hole at the line and, finding no white jerseys in front of him, carried the ball 87 yards to the end zone

On the Bulldogs' following possession, linebacker Jacob Cutrera intercepted Champion, and LSU needed just 42 seconds to make the score 44-7.

That was it for the Tigers' starters, as Coach Les Miles substituted entire offensive and defensive units for the remainder of the game. Bulldogs kicker Danny Horwedel managed to bang home a 38-yard field goal with 13:09 left to make it 44-10, but by then even the LSU student section and the much smaller contingent of Bulldogs fans had largely vanished.

TEAM	1ST	2ND	3RD	4TH	FINAL
La. Tech	0	0	7	3	10
LSU	10	17	17	14	58
Attendance					92,512 at Tiger Stadium

TEAM STATISTICS	LSU	LA TECH
FIRST DOWNS	22	15
RUSHES-YARDS	40-321	35-67
PASSING YARDS (NET)	274	189
PASSES (ATT-COMP-INT)	39-20-2	30-16-2
TOTAL OFFENSE (PLAYS-YARDS)	70-595	74-256
PENALTIES (NUMBER-YARDS)	8-60	6-75
PUNTS (NUMBER-AVERAGE)	3-42.7	7-43.1
PUNT RETURNS (NUMBER-YARDS-TD)	3-14-0	1-5-0
KICKOFF RETURNS (NUMBER-YARDS-TD)	2-38-0	10-318-0
POSSESSION TIME	28.46	31.14
SACKS BY (YARDS LOST)	2-12	2-16
FIELD GOALS (ATTEMPTED)	3-3	1-1
FUMBLES-LOST	0-0	3-3

SCORING SUMMARY

LSU   Matt Flynn 1-yard run (Colt David kick). Five plays, 24 yards in 1:39.
LSU   David 31-yard field goal. Four plays, 4 yards in 1:33.
LA TECH   Brian Jackson 37-yard pass from Zac Champion (Danny Horwedel). Two plays, 52 yards in 0:15.
LSU   David 44-yard field goal. Seven plays, 39 yards in 2:23.
LSU   Terrance Toliver 71-yard pass from Flynn (David kick). Three plays, 81 yards in 1:04.
LSU   Brandon LaFell 37-yard pass from Flynn (David kick). Three plays, 75 yards in 0:46.
LSU   David 28-yard field goal. Nine plays, 50 yards in 2:42.
LSU   Jacob Hester 87-yard run (David kick). Three plays, 94 yards in 0:59.
LSU   Richard Dickson 14-yard pass from Flynn (David kick). Three plays, 39 yards in 0:42.
LA TECH   Horwedel 38-yard field goal. Eleven plays, 38 yards in 2:26.
LSU   Trindon Holliday 15-yard run (David kick). Six plays, 72 yards in 3:29.
LSU   Mit Cole 2-yard pass from Ryan Perrilloux (David kick). Five plays, 45 yards in 2:21.

INDIVIDUAL OFFENSIVE STATISTICS

RUSHING   LSU — Jacob Hester 11-115; Richard Murphy 3-62; Trindon Holliday 5-45; Shawn Jordan 4-32; Keiland Williams 4-29; Terrance Toliver 1- 20.
LA TECH — Patrick Jackson 9-42; William Griffin 8-20; Zac Champion 8-7.

PASSING   LSU — Matt Flynn 26/14-3-2, 237; Ryan Perrilloux 4/2-1-0, 37.
LA TECH — Zac Champion 39/20-1-2, 189.

RECEIVING   LSU — Brandon LaFell 5-80; Terrance Toliver 3-119 ; Early Doucet 3-22.
LA TECH — Dustin Mitchell 5-29; William Griffin 3-20; Joe Anderson 3-13

INDIVIDUAL DEFENSIVE STATISTICS

INTERCEPTIONS   LSU — Jacob Cutrera 1; Jonathan Zenon 1.
LOUISIANA TECH — Deon Young 1; Shalama Walker 1.

SACKS   LSU — Glenn Dorsey 1; Kirston Pittman 1.
LOUISIANA TECH — Josh Muse 2.

TACKLES   LSU — Jacob Cutrera 7; Glenn Dorsey 7; Perry Riley 7; Kelvin Sheppard 7; Chris Hawkins 5; Drake Nevis 5; Craig Steltz 5; Curtis Taylor 5; Al Woods 5.
LOUISIANA TECH — Antonio Baker 12; Deon Young 10; Weldon Brown 7; Quin Harris 6; Tony Moss 5-0.

ap top 10

released 11.11.07

1 LSU	2 OREGON	3 KANSAS	4 OKLAHOMA	5 MISSOURI	6 WEST VIRGINIA	7 OHIO STATE	8 ARIZONA STATE	9 GEORGIA	10 VIRGINIA TECH
Avg.: .9802	.9383	.9094	.8540	.8096	.7863	.7744	.7500	.6724	.6133

Wide receiver Terrance Toliver scores on a 71-yard pass from Matt Flynn. STAFF PHOTO BY JOHN McCUSKER

1 LSU	2 OREGON	3 OKLAHOMA	4 KANSAS	5 WEST VIRGINIA	6 MISSOURI	7 OHIO STATE	8 GEORGIA	9 ARIZONA STATE	10 VIRGINIA TECH
First-place votes: 40	First-place votes: 22	First-place votes: 1	First-place votes: 1	First-place votes: 1					

ole miss

Tigers linebacker Ali Highsmith (7) and company make sure running back BenJarvus Green-Ellis doesn't get anywhere.
STAFF PHOTO BY CHUCK COOK

TIGERS | 41
REBELS | 24

11.17.07 | 2:30 p.m. | Vaught-Hemingway Stadium | Oxford, Miss.

tigers 41
rebels 24

BY JAMES VARNEY STAFF WRITER

A lthough LSU players and coaches dubbed it another ugly win, it was a win all the same for the No. 1-ranked Tigers, as they dispatched Ole Miss 41-24 in Oxford, Miss.

The touchdowns came in bunches early and late, but the game did not have the feel of a close one after sophomore wide receiver Trindon Holliday took a kickoff 98 yards for a touchdown in the first quarter to gave LSU (10-1, 6-1 Southeastern Conference) a lead it never relinquished. In fact, LSU built on that 14-7 lead, and while senior Ole Miss backup quarterback Brent Schaeffer gave the Tigers some headaches, the Rebels never pulled closer than two scores after the Tigers built a 21-7 lead early in the third quarter.

The victory gave LSU its first outright SEC Western Division crown. The previous times LSU represented the division in the SEC championship game it did so by virtue of tiebreakers.

While LSU Coach Les Miles found elements to fault in his team's performance, he said the win outweighed all else.

"Ole Miss banked everything it had on this, coming off its open week," Miles said. "We turned up the heat a little bit on them, but we've got to play better on defense, I can tell you that."

Ole Miss gained 466 yards on offense, and did so with a mix of runs and passes that kept LSU off-balance. LSU never fully contained Schaeffer, who accounted for more than 300 yards.

"He's a shifty guy, and we knew not to let him get outside," said LSU sophomore linebacker Jacob Cutrera, who had four tackles and jarred loose a fumble on the Tigers' 1-yard line to

Wide receiver Trindon Holliday quickly gets LSU back on
track by returning a kickoff 98 yards for a touchdown.
STAFF PHOTO BY CHUCK COOK

tigers 41 rebels 24

quell a Rebels' scoring chance. "But it happened a couple of times."

The Rebels, along with about two-thirds of those at Vaught-Hemingway Stadium, went into halftime thinking about what might have been after the first-quarter scoring blitz and some Ole Miss miscues. After LSU fifth-year senior quarterback Matt Flynn opened the scoring with a 5-yard touchdown run, Ole Miss senior tailback BenJarvus Green-Ellis fumbled the ball at LSU's 1 on Cutrera's hit.

When LSU was forced to punt out of its end zone on the subsequent possession, sophomore wide receiver Marshay Green lifted the Rebels' spirits. He caught the ball on the run at LSU's 44 and sprinted down the left side of the field and beat two Tigers to the pylon for a touchdown that tied the score at 7.

"We underkicked our coverage; we outran the ball," Miles said.

But the tie score held for just 14 seconds.

Holliday gathered the ensuing kickoff at the 2-yard line, got behind his wedge in the middle and squirted through to the other side. He cut to his left and, after eluding the desperate grab of the Ole Miss kicker, raced past the LSU sideline and went untouched into the end zone to make the score 14-7.

"I ran up behind the wedge, saw a crease and just hit it," Holliday said. "I told myself on the sideline I was going to come out and make a big play and change the momentum."

The electrifying play put LSU ahead to stay, and proved true the Tigers' coaching staff assessment that their return game was just millimeters from clicking on a big play. But it looked as if Ole Miss would tie the score again before halftime on a protracted drive marked by oddities.

Senior quarterback Seth Adams was benched in favor of Schaeffer, and his greater mobility gave the Tigers fits. Darting and scrambling, Schaeffer moved the Rebels down the field, including a conversion on third-and-29 on a pass to sophomore wide receiver Shay Hodge, who finished with 90 yards on four catches.

But the drive, on which Ole Miss Coach Ed Orgeron burned all three of his timeouts, stalled at LSU's 8, where

TEAM	1ST	2ND	3RD	4TH	FINAL
LSU	14	0	10	17	41
Ole Miss	7	0	3	14	24

Attendance 61,118 at Vaught-Hemingway Stadium

SCORING SUMMARY

LSU — Matt Flynn 5-yard run (Colt David kick). Eleven plays, 98 yards in 4:25.

OLE MISS — Marshay Green 44-yard punt return (Joshua Shene kick).

LSU — Trindon Holliday 98-yard kickoff return (David kick).

LSU — Keiland Williams 10-yard run (David kick). Ten plays, 54 yards in 4:50.

OLE MISS — Shene 23-yard field goal. Nine plays, 68 yards in 3:19.

LSU — David 48-yard field goal. Seven plays, 31 yards in 2:28.

LSU — David 43-yard field goal. Twelve plays, 66 yards in 5:25.

OLE MISS — Brent Schaeffer 38-yard run (Shene kick). Seven plays, 70 yards in 2:25.

LSU — Jacob Hester 2-yard run (David kick). Four plays, 20 yards in 1:20.

OLE MISS — Shay Hodge, 33-yard pass from Schaeffer (Shene kick). Four plays, 68 yards in 0:50.

LSU — Charles Scott 29-yard run (David kick). Two plays, 46 yards in 0:39.

TEAM STATISTICS

	LSU	OLE MISS
FIRST DOWNS	21	25
RUSHES-YARDS (NET)	40-228	28-201
PASSING YARDS	168	265
PASSES (ATT-COMP-INT)	25-17-0	39-17-3
TOTAL OFFENSE (PLAYS-YARDS)	65-396	67-466
PENALTIES (NUMBER-YARDS)	9-66	8-74
PUNTS (NUMBER-AVERAGE)	4-41.5	4-40.0
PUNT RETURNS (NUMBER-YARDS-TD)	0-0-0	2-49-1
KICKOFF RETURNS (NUMBER-YARDS-TD)	4-127-1	7-133-0
POSSESSION TIME	30:56	29:04
SACKS BY (YARDS LOST)	1-8	3-25
FIELD GOALS	2-2	1-1
FUMBLES-LOST	0-0	1-1

INDIVIDUAL OFFENSIVE STATISTICS

RUSHING LSU — Charles Scott 3-66; Jacob Hester 13-65; Keiland Williams 5-41; Trindon Holliday 4-25; Richard Murphy 3-17; Matt Flynn 12-14.
OLE MISS — Brent Schaeffer 8-94; BenJarvus Green-Ellis 12-53; Dexter McCluster 2-38; Bruce Hall 4-15; Seth Adams 2-1.

PASSING LSU — Matt Flynn 25/17-0-0, 168.
OLE MISS — Brent Schaeffer 28/13-1-2, 208; Seth Adams 11/4-0-1, 57.

RECEIVING LSU — Early Doucet 8-58; Brandon LaFell 3-19; Keiland Williams 2-38; Richard Murphy 1-21; Jacob Hester 1-14; Demetrius Byrd 1-11; Charles Scott 1-7.
OLE MISS — Dexter McCluster 5-73; Shay Hodge 4-90; Marshay Green 3-17; Jason Cook 2-14; Bruce Hall 1-35; Robert Hough 1-21; Michael Hicks 1-15.

INDIVIDUAL DEFENSIVE STATISTICS

INTERCEPTIONS LSU — Craig Steltz 2; Curtis Taylor 1.

SACKS LSU — Kirston Pittman 1.
OLE MISS — Greg Hardy 2; Vinciente DeLoach 1.

TACKLES LSU — Danny McCray 8; Curtis Taylor 8; Ali Highsmith 7; Craig Steltz 5; Jacob Cutrera 4; Chevis Jackson 4.
OLE MISS — Jamarca Sanford 10; Tony Fein 9; Jerry Peria 6-2; Cassius Vaughn 7; Johnny Brown 6, Dustin Mouzon 6.

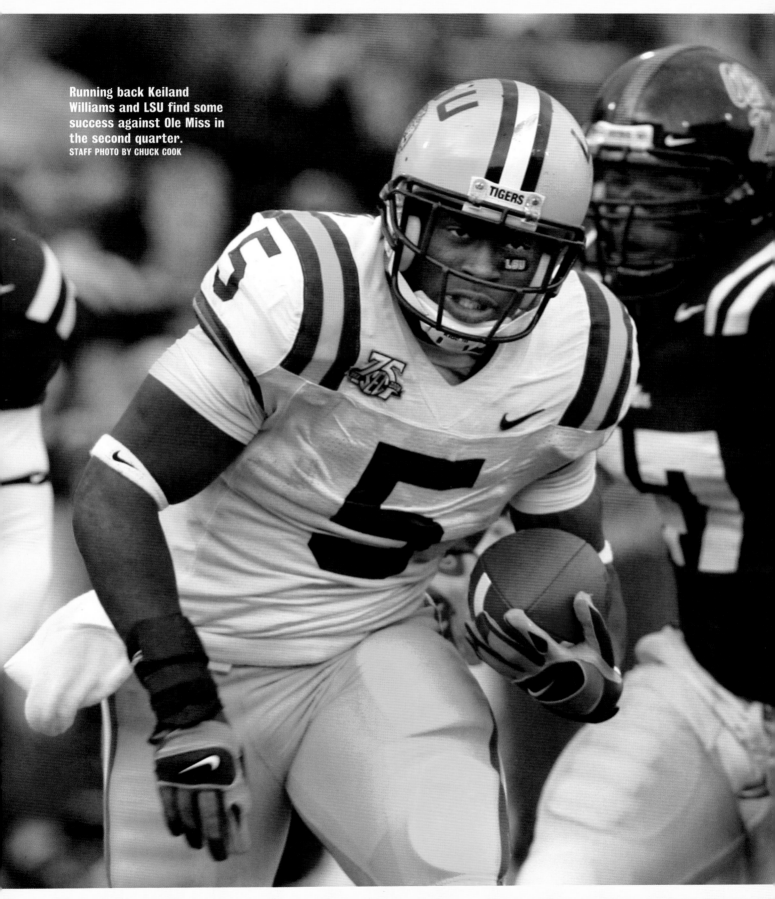

Running back Keiland Williams and LSU find some success against Ole Miss in the second quarter.
STAFF PHOTO BY CHUCK COOK

| Game 11 | 11.17.07 | Vaught-Hemingway Stadium |

tigers 41 | rebels 24

Schaeffer had scrambled for another first down. After each team had a 5-yard penalty on back-to-back plays — the second a delay of game against Ole Miss — Orgeron pulled Schaeffer and reinserted Adams. He said later he thought Schaeffer appeared "rattled" by the confusion.

However, with 25 seconds remaining in the half, Orgeron had cause to regret his decision when Adams threw a pass to the back of the end zone that senior safety Craig Steltz picked off, the first of his two interceptions.

LSU salted the game away on the opening possession of the second half when sophomore tailback Keiland Williams, who racked up nearly 80 yards on rushes and receptions, darted in on a 10-yard run to give the Tigers a two-touchdown lead.

Ole Miss' Joshua Shene kicked a 23-yard field goal to trim the margin to 21-10, but David had kicks from 48 and 43 yards to make it 27-10 with 11:36 remaining. The teams tacked on 28 more points before the final gun.

The Rebels got touchdowns via Schaeffer's legs, when he scampered 38 yards for a score, and his arm on a 33-yard pass to Shay in the corner of the end zone with 2:54 remaining.

Sandwiched between those scores, however, were two more LSU touchdowns. The first was a 2-yard bull by Jacob Hester after Steltz's second interception and a personal foul on Ole Miss set up LSU on the Rebels' 20. The second came on a brilliant run by Charles Scott, who kept his balance after stumbling in the flat and took it 29 yards for the final score. Scott finished with 66 yards on three carries.

Tigers running back Charles Scott wears down an already tired Rebels' defense in the fourth quarter.
STAFF PHOTO BY CHUCK COOK

ap top 10
released 11.18.07

| **1** LSU First-place votes: 60 | **2** KANSAS First-place votes: 3 | **3** MISSOURI First-place votes: 1 | **4** WEST VIRGINIA | **5** OHIO STATE | **6** GEORGIA | **7** ARIZONA STATE | **8** VIRGINIA TECH | **9** OREGON | **10** OKLAHOMA |

lsu's 2007 championship season **87**

arkansas

After the Razorbacks scored a touchdown against the No. 1-ranked Tigers in the third overtime, running back Felix Jones dives in for the two-point conversion. STAFF PHOTO BY DAVID GRUNFELD

RAZORBACKS 50
TIGERS 48 3OT

11.23.07 | 1:30 p.m. | Tiger Stadium | Baton Rouge, La.

razorbacks 50 tigers 48

BY JAMES VARNEY STAFF WRITER

A touchdown in the final minute to cap a monumental drive — typical LSU game.

But this time it proved atypical. That touchdown was only good enough for a tie, and a season marked by one magical comeback after another ended in ashes for the Tigers. In its final regular-season game, LSU fell to Arkansas 50-48 in triple overtime in Baton Rouge.

The loss seemed as if it would sound the death knell for the Tigers' national championship hopes. No. 1 LSU (10-2, 6-2 Southeastern Conference) was sure to drop in the polls and the BCS standings, and chaos would once again engulf the college football world as the national championship game drew closer.

A state of shock seemed to settle over the fans packed into Tiger Stadium when, on the final play — LSU's required attempt for a two-point conversion in triple overtime — fifth-year senior Matt Flynn's pass was intercepted in the back of the end zone.

LSU Coach Les Miles was tight-lipped afterward, but he insisted the Tigers would recover against Tennessee at the SEC championship game the next week at the Georgia Dome in Atlanta.

"We still look forward to playing another game, a very big game, " Miles said. "But you ain't going to motivate a team tonight. Tonight, you are just going to be sick."

The Razorbacks (8-4, 4-4) endured a similar situation last season when, having sewn up the Western Division crown, they lost to the Tigers 31-26. But that defeat carried none of the gloomy baggage that weighed down LSU.

Arkansas junior tailback Darren McFadden shredded LSU's defense for 211 yards and three touchdowns.

LSU entered the game with the SEC's top-ranked rushing

LSU wide receiver Chris Mitchell is unable to hold onto a pass thrown by quarterback Matt Flynn.
STAFF PHOTO BY CHUCK COOK

| Game 12 | 11.23.07 | Tiger Stadium |

razorbacks 50   tigers 48

defense and the fourth best in the country. The Razorbacks rushed for 385 yards and had four backs who averaged 5.0 yards or better per carry.

Among the Arkansas backs who hurt LSU was senior full-back Peyton Hillis, who rushed for two touchdowns and caught two more. Hillis also made one of the key plays, finding himself wide open on fourth-and-10 from the 25-yard line in the first overtime — after LSU already had scored a touchdown — and hauling in a pass from junior quarterback Casey Dick for a first down. Arkansas gained 513 yards on an LSU defense Miles said was "worn thin."

Those totals overshadowed another fine performance by LSU senior running Jacob Hester, who had 28 carries for 126 yards and two touchdowns in his curtain call at Tiger Stadium.

Hester and Miles praised the play of LSU fifth-year senior quarterback Matt Flynn, who threw for 209 yards and three touchdowns. However, Flynn completed only 22 of 47 passes, and the Tigers' passing attack was ineffective for long stretches.

TEAM	1ST	2ND	3RD	4TH	1OT	2OT	3OT	FINAL
Arkansas	0	7	14	7	7	7	8	**50**
LSU	6	0	15	7	7	7	6	**48**

Attendance   92,606 at Tiger Stadium

TEAM STATISTICS

TEAM STATISTICS	LSU	ARKANSAS
FIRST DOWNS	25	21
RUSHES-YARDS (NET)	48-204	53-385
PASSING YARDS (NET)	209	128
PASSES (ATT-COMP-INT)	47-22-0	24-13-0
TOTAL OFFENSE (PLAYS-YARDS)	95-413	77-513
PENALTIES (NUMBER-YARDS)	4-35	9-62
PUNTS (NUMBER-AVERAGE)	8-42.4	7-36.4
PUNT RETURNS (NUMBER-YARDS-TD)	2-11-0	3-3-0
KICKOFF RETURNS (NUMBER-YARDS-TD)	5-104-0	6-122-0
POSSESSION	31:27	28:33
SACKS BY (YARDS LOST)	0-0	1-7
FIELD GOALS (ATTEMPTED-MADE)	2-2	0-0
FUMBLES-LOST	3-0	3-1

SCORING SUMMARY

LSU — Colt David 32-yard field goal. Seven plays, 11 yards in 1:35.
LSU — David 49-yard field goal. Eleven plays, 41 yards in 4:31.
ARK — Darren McFadden 16-yard run (Alex Tejada kick). Nine plays, 97 yards in 3:23.
ARK — McFadden 73-yard run (Tejada kick). Five plays, 80 yards in 1:46.
LSU — Jacob Hester 12-yard run (Two-point conversion). Eight plays, 51 yards in 1:52.
ARK — Peyton Hillis 65-yard run (Tejada kick). Four plays, 83 yards in 1:54.
LSU — Demetrius Byrd 7-yard pass from Flynn (David kick). Ten plays, 75 yards in 3:18.
ARK — Hillis 24-yard pass from McFadden (Tejada kick). Six plays, 72 yards in 2:24.
LSU — Byrd 2-yard pass from Flynn (David kick). Thirteen plays, 79 yards in 4:02.
LSU — Flynn 12-yard run (David kick). Three plays, 25 yards.
ARK — Hillis 10-yard pass from Casey Dick (Tejada kick). Seven plays, 25 yards.
ARK — McFadden 9-yard run (Tejada kick). Two plays, 25 yards.
LSU — Hester 2-yard run (David kick). Five plays, 25 yards.
ARK — Hillis 3-yard run (Two-point conversion). Six plays, 25 yards.
LSU — Brandon LaFell pass from Flynn (Two-point conversion pass intercepted). Three plays, 25 yards.

INDIVIDUAL OFFENSIVE STATISTICS

RUSHING   LSU — Jacob Hester 28-126; Keiland Williams 10-47; Matt Flynn 9-27; Charles Scott 1-4.
ARKANSAS — Darren McFadden 32-211; Peyton Hillis 11-89; Felix Jones 9-89; London Crawford 1-5.

PASSING   LSU — Matt Flynn 47/22-3-0, 209.
ARKANSAS — Casey Dick 18/10-1-0, 94; Darren McFadden 6/3-1-0, 34.

RECEIVING   LSU — Early Doucet 7-52; Demetrius Byrd 6-46; Richard Dickson 5-69; Brandon LaFell 3-22; Charles Scott 1-20.
ARKANSAS — Peyton Hillis 5-62; Marcus Monk 2-12; Felix Jones 2-10.

INDIVIDUAL DEFENSIVE STATISTICS

SACKS   ARKANSAS — Freddie Fairchild 1.

TACKLES   LSU — Ali Highsmith 19; Craig Steltz 16; Darry Beckwith 11; Glenn Dorsey 6; Chad Jones 5; Drake Nevis 5; Luke Sanders 5.
ARKANSAS — Matt Hewitt 16; Matterral Richardson 11; Freddie Fairchild 11; Kevin Woods 9; Weston Dacus 8; Marcus Harrison 8; Adrian Davis 7.

After losing to Arkansas in triple overtime Tigers quarterback Matt Flynn sits in despair.
STAFF PHOTO BY DAVID GRUNFELD

1 MISSOURI	2 WEST VIRGINIA	3 OHIO STATE	4 GEORGIA	5 LSU	6 VIRGINIA TECH	7 KANSAS	8 USC	9 OKLAHOMA	10 FLORIDA
First-place votes: 45	First-place votes: 20	First-place votes: 1							

lsu's 2007 championship season 93

Jonathan Zenon picks off a pass by Tennessee quarterback Erik Ainge and returns it 19 yards for a touchdown in the fourth quarter.
STAFF PHOTO BY MICHAEL DeMOCKER

TIGERS 21
VOLS 14

12.01.07 | 3 p.m. | Georgia Dome | Atlanta, Ga.

Backup quarterback Ryan Perrilloux got the start for LSU because of Matt Flynn's injury. He didn't disappoint, completing 20 of 30 passes with one touchdown.
STAFF PHOTO BY CHUCK COOK

tigers 21 vols 14

BY JAMES VARNEY STAFF WRITER

Capping off one of the most tumultuous days in athletics at LSU, Coach Les Miles said he had no intention of leaving the Tigers, and then his team proceeded to win the Southeastern Conference championship by defeating Tennessee 21-14.

LSU showed flashes of the team it will field next season, as sophomore backup quarterback Ryan Perrilloux played superbly, connecting with wide receivers Brandon LaFell, a sophomore, and Demetrius Byrd, a junior, in critical situations. Perrilloux, who started instead of injured fifth-year senior Matt Flynn, was chosen the game's Most Valuable Player.

Perrilloux completed 20 of 30 passes with one touchdown and one interception. The Tigers' offensive production was bolstered by running back Jacob Hester, who added yet another scintillating game to his résumé, gaining 120 yards on 23 carries.

Despite LSU's undeniable talent, the SEC championship came no easier to the Tigers than most of their other wins this season. By halftime, it seemed the Tigers would have the game in control, given they held the ball for more than 21 minutes and had nearly triple Tennessee's yardage, 271 to 93.

After scoring a touchdown on its opening drive on an 11-yard pass from senior quarterback Erik Ainge to senior tight end Chris Brown, the Volunteers mustered just two first downs the rest of the half.

But LSU, in turn, mustered only two field goals (both 30 yards) by junior Colt David in the first quarter, and David jerked another 30-yard attempt wide right with six seconds remaining in the half that would have given LSU the lead.

Perrilloux threw the ball successfully downfield when

tigers 21 | vols 14

Jonathan Zenon's teammates mob the LSU cornerback after he returned an interception for a game-winning touchdown.
STAFF PHOTO BY MICHAEL DeMOCKER

given time, and the Tigers churned out yardage, but drives were cut short with penalties or big losses.

In one series, Perrilloux threw a pass to Byrd for a first down at LSU's 30-yard line. On the next play, however, sophomore Keiland Williams was stuffed on the left side but, rather than going down for a short loss, he tried to turn it into a big play. Pushed further backward, Williams reversed field and eventually was upended for a 14-yard loss.

On the next play, Perrilloux was sacked, and LSU, with the predominately pro-Tennessee crowd roaring, wound up punting out of the back of its end zone on fourth-and-36. A fine kick by senior Patrick Fisher bailed LSU out, however, and Tennessee had to punt three plays later.

LSU finally grabbed the lead, 13-7, on the opening drive of the second half.

On a third down, Perrilloux bought himself a second of extra time, and then tossed the ball downfield to LaFell, who raced to Tennessee's 21 for a 48-yard gain. After a reverse to senior wide receiver Early Doucet lost 10 yards, LSU faced a third-and-16. Perrilloux drilled a pass through a seam in the deep left side of the Volunteers' secondary that Byrd caught for a 27-yard touchdown.

Tennessee's leader, Ainge, finally found some rhythm after Byrd's score. But after the Volunteers' Daniel Lincoln missed a 30-yard field goal, it looked as if LSU was driving for what may have been the deciding score when Trindon Holliday, darting up the middle, inexplicably popped the ball up in the air. Tennessee recovered, and the momentum shifted perceptibly. LSU never seemed the same team thereafter.

Ainge, working out of a no-huddle format, found a comfortable rhythm on the subsequent drive and picked LSU's secondary apart. On third-and-goal from the 6, he rifled a pass to wide receiver Josh Briscoe, who caught it near the goal line with safety Danny McCray draped around him. Briscoe won the battle for the ball, McCray fell down, and Tennessee was back on top 14-13 with 3:09 remaining in the third quarter.

Hardly had LSU's defense left the field, it seemed, than a Perrilloux pass into no-man's land over the middle was intercepted by Eric Berry. Tennessee could not get a first

| Southeastern Conference Championship |
| 12.01.07 | Georgia Dome |
tigers 21 | vols 14

down, however, and Tennessee Coach Phillip Fulmer elected to have Lincoln attempt a 52-yard kick that sailed wide right.

With less than 13 minutes remaining, Miles called for a fake punt that gave LSU a first down inside Tennessee territory. But yet another penalty — LSU's eighth — forced a punt that Fisher managed to get down just inside Tennessee's 10-yard line. On third-and 5, Ainge made a fateful blunder.

He tried a long throw into the right flat, and LSU senior cornerback Jonathan Zenon stepped in front of a Volunteers receiver at the 18-yard line. Zenon intercepted the pass on a dead run and raced untouched into the end zone, sending the LSU faithful into a frenzy.

LSU decided to go for the two-point conversion, and Perrilloux faked a handoff to Hester and darted up the middle on a quarterback draw. The play was successful, giving the Tigers a 21-14 lead.

Ainge brought the Volunteers back, but on third-and-4 from LSU's 21 he overthrew Denarius Moore, and Fulmer elected to go for it on fourth down. On the identical play, Ainge's throw was slightly behind Moore, and he could not hold on.

Again, the Vols stuffed LSU, and again Ainge brought them back. With 4:10 remaining, Tennessee began a drive on its 33-yard line, and on second-and-17 Ainge hit tailback Arian Foster on a screen that broke for 47 yards. On the next play, however, Ainge's pass across the middle was intercepted by linebacker Darry Beckwith.

With 1:35 remaining, Hester took a pitch, gained 20 yards, which gave him more than 1,000 yards for his senior season, and sealed the crown. 🐯

LSU coach Les Miles called for a fake punt on fourth down against the Volunteers in the fourth quarter. Punter Patrick Fisher completed a pass to fullback Quinn Johnson (45) for a first down.
STAFF PHOTO BY MICHAEL DeMOCKER

ap top 10
released 12.02.07

1 OHIO STATE	2 LSU	3 OKLAHOMA	4 GEORGIA	5 VIRGINIA TECH	6 USC	7 MISSOURI	8 KANSAS	9 FLORIDA	10 HAWAII
First-place votes: 50	First-place votes: 11	First-place votes: 1	First-place votes: 1	First-place votes: 1					First-place votes: 1

lsu's 2007 championship season 101

Wide receiver Demetrius Byrd (2) celebrates catching a 27-yard touchdown pass with wide receiver Brandon LaFell (1). STAFF PHOTO BY CHUCK COOK

TEAM	1ST	2ND	3RD	4TH	FINAL
TENNESSEE	7	0	7	0	14
LSU	6	0	7	8	21

Attendance — 73,832 at the Georgia Dome, Atlanta

SCORING SUMMARY

TENN — Chris Brown 11-yard pass from Erik Ainge (Daniel Lincoln kick). Six plays, 62 yards in 3:00.

LSU — Colt David 30-yard field goal. Ten plays, 63 yards in 3:31.

LSU — David 30-yard goal. Nine plays, 58 yards in 3:57.

LSU — Demetrius Byrd 27-yard pass from Ryan Perrilloux (David kick). Six plays, 76 yards in 3:08.

Tenn — Josh Briscoe 6-yard pass from Erik Ainge (Lincoln kick). Nine plays, 66 yards in 3:40.

LSU — Jonathan Zenon 18-yard interception return (Perrilloux rushed for the two-point conversion).

TEAM STATISTICS

	LSU	TENNESSEE
FIRST DOWNS	21	17
RUSHES-YARDS (NET)	47-212	26-94
PASSING YARDS (NET)	252	249
PASSES (ATT-COMP-INT)	33-21-1	40-20-2
TOTAL OFFENSE (PLAYS-YARDS)	80-464	66-343
PENALTIES (NUMBER-YARDS)	9-44	0-0
PUNTS (NUMBER-AVERAGE)	4-45.0	5-36.0
PUNT RETURNS (NUMBER-YARDS-TD)	1-1-0	2-11-0
KICKOFF RETURNS (NUMBER-YARDS-TD)	3-64-0	4-99-0
POSSESSION TIME	36:08	23:52
SACKS BY (YARDS LOST)	0-0	1-8
FIELD GOALS (ATTEMPTED-MADE)	3-2	2-0
FUMBLES-LOST	3-1	2-0

INDIVIDUAL OFFENSIVE STATISTICS

RUSHING — LSU — Jacob Hester 23-120; Trindon Holliday 6-58; Keiland Williams 5-34; Ryan Perrilloux 9-14; Richard Murphy 1-0; Early Doucet 1 minus-10. TENNESSEE — Arian Foster 21-55; Gerald Jones 2-39; Lennon Creer 1-1; Jonathan Crompton 1-0.

PASSING — LSU — Ryan Perrilloux 30/20-1-1, 243; Patrick Fisher 1/1-0-0, 9. TENNESSEE — Erik Ainge 40/20-2-2, 249.

RECEIVING — LSU — Early Doucet 5-29; Demetrius Byrd 4-72; Brandon LaFell 3-65; Richard Dickson 2-15; Richard Murphy 2-14; Jacob Hester 2-5; Keith Zinger 1-27; Charles Scott 1-16; Quinn Johnson 1-9. TENNESSEE — Josh Briscoe 8-79; Arian Foster 2-40; Chris Brown 2-35; Brad Cottam 2-28; Lucas Taylor 2-25; Austin Rogers 2-20; Denarius Moore 1-16; Lennon Creer 1-6.

INDIVIDUAL DEFENSIVE STATISTICS

INTERCEPTIONS — LSU — Darry Beckwith 1; Jonathan Zenon 1. TENNESSEE — Eric Berry 1.

SACKS — TENNESSEE — Nevin McKenzie 1.

TACKLES — LSU — Craig Steltz 8; Ali Highsmith 7; Chad Jones 6; Jonathan Zenon 6; Chevis Jackson 5; Danny McCray 5. TENNESSEE — Jerod Mayo 15; Jonathan Hefney 10; Rico McCoy 8; Xavier Mitchell 8; Eric Berry 7.

Coach Miles shows true colors by staying

PETER FINNEY

A funny thing happened at the Georgia Dome.

There was this soap opera, "As The Les Miles World Turns, " that looked like it was going to go on all day.

Suddenly, a football game broke out.

So did an SEC championship

So, apparently, did the Ryan Perrilloux era.

And what do you know?

Perrilloux, a sophomore who began the day as backup quarterback, played his way to the top of the depth chart.

That's because he ended the day as the MVP in a 21-14 victory over Tennessee, handing his 33-victory, 6-loss head coach his first championship over the finest three-year stretch in school history.

So what about Miles?

Well, he began the day as coach of the LSU Tigers.

And he will begin the 2008 football season in the same job.

With a pay raise.

Raising the question: How much is Miles worth to LSU?

Next year he'll be worth a reported $2.6 million a year, up from the $1.85 million he was paid this year.

It was all part of a revamped new contract hammered out Friday night, one with the usual sweeteners based on accomplishments.

How could ESPN report that Miles, without a doubt, was headed for Michigan?

My guess is its sources, as is usual with stories involving coaching changes, had something to do with Miles' agent, not Miles, someone completely involved with getting his team ready to play for a conference championship.

At times like this, you hear all kinds of stories/speculation.

I heard, for example, Michigan's "unofficial" offer to Miles was close to "insulting."

LSU Coach Les Miles celebrates along with players and coaches after the Tigers won the Southeastern Conference championship at the Georgia Dome in Atlanta.
STAFF PHOTO BY CHUCK COOK

| Southeastern Championship Game |
| 12.01.07 | Georgia Dome |
tigers 21 | vols 14

While I can understand Miles going public several hours before Saturday's kickoff, he could have done a better job telling it like it was: "I agreed to a new contract Friday night."

Period.

After winning a conference championship, Miles was more focused on the matter at hand. He spoke from the heart.

He'll always be "a Michigan man."

But he, and his family, are where they want to be. "This is home," he said

Les Miles realized, as a football coach, he was saying good-bye to his alma mater.

First Jonathan Zenon is picking off Erik Ainge for the go-ahead points, then Darry Beckwith is saving the day with another pick as the Vols were threatening to send it into overtime.

It has been like that all year for a roller-coaster football team that led the SEC in penalties, a sign of a lack of discipline that has driven Tiger fans up the wall.

More often than not, for a team that has gone to the post favorite in every game, Miles' bunch kept finding a way.

Winning the SEC championship was a huge step, financially, for someone still sitting in the shadow of his predecessor.

And, when you get down to the nitty-gritty, Saturday's soap opera had something to do with the sunshine cloud created by Nick Saban.

The color of a sunshine cloud is green.

Dark green.

At times like this, you hear all kinds of stories/speculation. I heard, for example, Michigan's "unofficial" offer to Miles was close to "insulting." While I can understand Miles going public several hours before Saturday's kickoff, he could have done a better job telling it like it was: "I agreed to a new contract Friday night." Period.

Forever.

A good decision?

You can look at it two ways.

At LSU, he's in a position to lock up a treasure throve of talent, more than he could ever hope to do, year to year, at Michigan, increasing his chances in the march to No. 1.

On the other hand, at LSU, he's going to battle in college football's toughest conference, where an unbeaten season, nowadays, is close to an impossible dream.

As you reflect on the immediate past, Miles' 2007 Tigers might have come as close as you can.

Against Kentucky, a game-winning field-goal attempt goes wide by less than a yard at the end of regulation.

Against Arkansas, the defense could not make what would have been a game-winning stop on fourth-and-10 in overtime.

On Saturday, the same defense came up with two of the biggest stops of the season, the kind that figures to embellish the resume of coordinator Bo Pelini as he heads to become the boss of the Nebraska Cornhuskers.

It began after the 2004 regular season, the day the owner of the Miami Dolphins flew to Baton Rouge in his private jet and offered the coach of the LSU Tigers the keys to the kingdom, complete control of the football operation, at a salary of, give or take a few bucks, $4 million a year.

Financially, it changed the landscape.

It's why Iowa's Kirk Ferentz is the top-salaried coach in the Big Ten, not because he won championships, but because he was offered a hefty raise by the Chicago Bears and Iowa wanted to keep him.

It's why Auburn's Tommy Tuberville has been offered a new contract that will pay him $2.8 million next season and an automatic $200,000 annual raise the next five years.

While money may not have been the primary reason Les Miles bid farewell to Ann Arbor, Mich., he obviously welcomes the challenge working at a school willing to pay what it takes to compete with a group of the highest-salaried college coaches in the business.

Can't argue with that.

Running back
Arian Foster feels the
wrath of LSU's defense,
which held Tennessee
to 94 yards rushing
on 26 carries.
STAFF PHOTO BY MICHAEL DeMOCKER

2007 statistics

INDIVIDUAL OFFENSIVE STATISTICS

RUSHING

PLAYER	GP	ATT	GAIN	LOSS	NET	AVG	TD	LNG	AVG/GAME
Jacob Hester	13	204	1032	15	1017	5.0	11	87	78.2
K. Williams	13	68	493	35	458	6.7	6	67	35.2
Trindon Holliday	12	50	368	17	351	7.0	2	33	29.2
Charles Scott	13	43	324	6	318	7.4	5	55	24.5
Matt Flynn	11	88	376	169	207	2.4	4	22	18.8
Ryan Perrilloux	11	51	253	50	203	4.0	2	23	18.5
Richard Murphy	13	33	207	10	197	6.0	2	53	15.2
Terrance Toliver	13	3	37	1	36	12.0	0	20	2.8
Shawn Jordan	13	4	32	0	32	8.0	0	15	2.5
Andrew Hatch	2	4	27	0	27	6.8	0	11	13.5
Brandon LaFell	13	1	18	0	18	18.0	1	18	1.4
Colt David	13	1	15	0	15	15.0	1	15	1.2
Early Doucet	9	1	0	10	-10	-10.0	0	0	-1.1
Team	7	12	0	23	-23	-1.9	0	0	-3.3
Total	13	563	3,182	336	2,846	5.1	34	87	218.9
Opponents	13	434	1,719	379	1,340	3.1	13	73	103.1

PASSING

PLAYER	GP	EFF.	CMP-ATT-INT	PCT	YARDS	TD	LNG	AVG/GAME
Matt Flynn	11	122.49	183-332-10	55.1	2,233	17	71	203.0
Ryan Perrilloux	11	175.59	51-75-2	68.0	694	8	62	63.1
Team	7	0.00	0-4-0	0.0	0	0	0	0.0
Andrew Hatch	2	87.80	1-2-0	50.0	9	0	9	4.5
Early Doucet	9	394.00	1-1-0	100.0	35	0	35	3.9
Patrick Fisher	13	175.60	1-1-0	100.0	9	0	9	0.7
Total	13	131.52	237-415-12	57.1	2,980	25	71	229.2
Opponents	13	96.12	197-425-21	46.4	2,350	17	67	180.8

RECEIVING

PLAYER	GP	NO	YARDS	AVG	TD	LNG	AVG/GAME
Early Doucet	9	50	474	9.5	4	34	52.7
Brandon LaFell	13	48	641	13.4	3	56	49.3
Demetrius Byrd	13	33	593	18.0	7	62	45.6
Richard Dickson	13	28	331	11.8	3	35	25.5
Jacob Hester	13	14	106	7.6	1	28	8.2
Jared Mitchell	11	13	143	11.0	0	32	13.0
Charles Scott	13	11	99	9.0	2	20	7.6
Terrance Toliver	13	10	249	24.9	3	71	19.2
K. Williams	13	8	114	14.2	1	46	8.8
Richard Murphy	13	8	74	9.2	0	21	5.7
Chris Mitchell	10	5	56	11.2	0	16	5.6
Keith Zinger	13	2	33	16.5	0	27	2.5
Quinn Johnson	13	2	18	9.0	0	13	1.4
Trindon Holliday	12	2	3	1.5	0	3	0.2
Matt Flynn	11	1	35	35.0	0	35	3.2
Ricky Dixon	5	1	9	9.0	0	9	1.8
Mit Cole	12	1	2	2.0	0	2	0.2
Total	13	237	2,980	12.6	25	71	229.2
Opponents	13	197	2,350	11.9	17	67	180.8

FIELD GOALS

PLAYER	FGM-FGA	PCT	1-19	20-29	30-39	40-49	50-60	LNG	BLKD
Colt David	25-32	78.1	0-0	7-7	12-15	6-9	0-1	49	1

PUNT RETURNS

PLAYER	NO	YARDS	AVG	TD	LONG
Chad Jones	16	104	6.5	0	16
Jared Mitchell	4	19	4.8	0	8
Trindon Holliday	1	0	0.0	0	0
Early Doucet	1	5	5.0	0	5
Total	22	128	5.8	0	16
Opponents	21	199	9.5	2	61

KICK RETURNS

PLAYER	NO	YARDS	AVG	TD	LONG
Trindon Holliday	18	468	26.0	1	98
Keiland Williams	10	199	19.9	0	25
Chad Jones	4	90	22.5	0	33
Kelvin Sheppard	2	12	6.0	0	11
Shawn Jordan	2	13	6.5	0	10
Lazarius Levingston	1	2	2.0	0	2
R.J. Jackson	1	0	0.0	0	0
Early Doucet	1	18	18.0	0	18
Jared Mitchell	1	3	3.0	0	3
Total	40	805	20.1	1	98
Opponents	87	1785	20.5	0	76

TOTAL OFFENSE

PLAYER	G	PLAYS	RUSH	PASS	TOTAL	AVG/GAME
Matt Flynn	11	420	207	2,233	2,440	221.8
Jacob Hester	13	204	1,017	0	1,017	78.2
Ryan Perrilloux	11	126	203	694	897	81.5
Keiland Williams	13	68	458	0	458	35.2
Trindon Holliday	12	50	351	0	351	29.2
Charles Scott	13	43	318	0	318	24.5
Richard Murphy	13	33	197	0	197	15.2
Andrew Hatch	2	6	27	9	36	18.0
Terrance Toliver	13	3	36	0	36	2.8
Shawn Jordan	13	4	32	0	32	2.5
Early Doucet	9	2	-10	35	25	2.8
Brandon LaFell	13	1	18	0	18	1.4
Colt David	13	1	15	0	15	1.2
Patrick Fisher	13	1	0	9	9	0.7
Total	13	978	2,846	2,980	5,826	448.2
Opponents	13	859	1,340	2,350	3,690	283.8

PUNTING

PLAYER	NO	YDS	AVG	LNG	TB	FC	I20	BLKD
Patrick Fisher	56	2,457	43.9	61	13	8	12	0
Team	1	22	22.0	22	0	0	0	1
Josh Jasper	1	40	40.0	40	0	1	1	0
Total	58	2,519	43.4	61	13	9	13	1
Opponents	79	3,093	39.2	59	4	20	25	0

KICKOFFS

PLAYER	NO	YDS	AVG	TB	OB	RET	NET	AVG YD
Josh Jasper	39	2,301	59.0	1	1	-	-	-
Andrew Crutchfield	33	2,078	63.0	1	0	-	-	-
Sean Gaudet	18	1,100	61.1	0	1	-	-	-
Colt David	2	119	59.5	0	0	-	-	-
Patrick Fisher	1	47	47.0	0	0	-	-	-
Total	93	5,645	60.7	2	2	1785	41.1	28
Opponents	46	2,692	58.5	3	1	805	39.7	30

SELECT PLAYER HONORS

DARRY BECKWITH, LB
- First-team All-SEC

COLT DAVID, PK
- First-team All-SEC

GLENN DORSEY, DT
- Outland Trophy winner
- Lombardi Award winner
- Lott Trophy winner
- Nagurski Award winner
- Bednarik Award finalist
- First-team All-America
  AP, AFCA, FWAA, Walter Camp Foundation, CBSSports.com, CNNSI.com, Rivals.com, Sporting News
- SEC Defensive Player of the Year
- First-team All-SEC

PATRICK FISHER, P
- First-team All-SEC

MATT FLYNN, QB
- SEC Offensive Player of the Week
  Oct. 20 vs. Auburn

JACOB HESTER, RB
- Second-team All-SEC
- SEC Offensive Player of the Week
  Oct. 6 vs. Florida

ALI HIGHSMITH, LB
- First-team All-America CBSSports.com
- Second-team All-America AP
- First-team All-SEC

CHEVIS JACKSON, CB
- First-team All-SEC

HERMAN JOHNSON, OG
- First-team All-SEC

CHAD JONES, S
- First-team Freshman All-America
  Sporting News
- Honorable mention Freshman All-America
  CollegeFootballNews.com
- Freshman All-SEC

RYAN PERRILLOUX, QB
- SEC championship game MVP
  Dec. 1 vs. Tennessee

KIRSTON PITTMAN, DE
- SEC Defensive Lineman of the Week
  Sept. 8 vs. Virginia Tech

CRAIG STELTZ, S
- First-team All-America
  AP, Walter Camp Foundation, CBSSports.com, CNNSI.com, Rivals.com
- First-team All-SEC

TERRANCE TOLIVER, WR
- Honorable mention Freshman All-America Sporting News
- Freshman All-SEC
  coaches, Rivals.com

STAFF PHOTO BY DAVID GRUNFELD

INDIVIDUAL DEFENSIVE STATISTICS

LEADERS

PLAYER	GP	SOLO	ASST	TTL	TFL-YDS	SCKS (No.-yds)	INT-YDS	BRUP	HURR	FUM Rcv.-Yds	FRCD FUM
Craig Steltz	13	66	31	97	5.0-20	1.0-8	6-153	7	-	1-0	3
Ali Highsmith	13	54	39	93	7.5-21	1.5-9	-	8	9	1-0	1
Glenn Dorsey	13	39	25	64	11.5-48	6.0-40	-	4	4	-	-
Darry Beckwith	11	36	27	63	6.5-26	1.5-14	1-0	4	2	1-0	-
Kirston Pittman	13	28	33	61	12.5-70	7.0-47	1-0	1	14	-	-
Danny McCray	13	49	12	61	4.0-33	3.0-32	2-0	3	1	1-0	-
Curtis Taylor	13	30	19	49	1.0-6	1.0-6	2-22	6	1	1-0	-
Chevis Jackson	13	32	10	42	3.0-7	-	4-18	15	-	-	-
Jonathan Zenon	13	28	13	41	1.5-2	-	3-42	7	-	1-0	1
Tyson Jackson	13	16	19	35	3.5-14	2.5-11	-	10	15	-	-
Chad Jones	13	26	8	34	3.0-32	2.0-25	1-0	3	-	-	1
Luke Sanders	13	13	15	28	1.5-10	0.5-7	-	3	5	1-0	1
Marlon Favorite	10	16	12	28	1.0-1	-	-	-	5	-	-
Perry Riley	13	8	14	22	1.5-10	0.5-6	-	-	-	-	-
Al Woods	11	13	9	22	2.0-15	2.0-15	-	-	1	3-0	-
Jacob Cutrera	11	11	10	21	1.5-3	-	1-9	1	1	-	1
Kelvin Sheppard	13	15	6	21	2.0-4	-	-	1	-	-	2
Drake Nevis	7	10	7	17	2.0-6	-	-	2	-	-	-
Harry Coleman	12	10	6	16	0.5-2	-	-	-	-	-	-
Chris Hawkins	12	12	1	13	-	-	-	3	-	-	-
T. Johnson	12	3	8	11	1.5-3	1.0-2	-	-	3	-	-
Charles Scott	13	7	2	9	-	-	-	-	-	1-0	-
Rahim Alem	11	7	1	8	4.0-19	2.0-17	-	-	1	-	1
L. Levingston	13	3	5	8	1.5-8	1.0-7	-	-	-	-	-
R.J. Jackson	13	6	2	8	-	-	-	-	-	-	-
Jacob Hester	13	4	4	8	-	-	-	-	-	1-0	1
Richard Murphy	13	4	4	8	-	-	-	-	-	-	-
Jai Eugene	11	4	3	7	-	-	-	-	1	-	-
Charles Alexander	3	3	3	6	-	-	-	-	2	-	-
Anthony Zehyoue	2	3	1	4	-	-	-	-	-	-	-
Jeremy Benton	4	1	2	3	-	-	-	-	-	-	-
R Jean-Francois	1	2	1	3	-	-	-	-	-	-	-
Brandon LaFell	13	2	1	3	-	-	-	-	-	-	-
A. Crutchfield	10	1	1	2	-	-	-	-	-	-	-
Team	13	10	1	10							
Total	13	572	355	927	78-360	32-246	21-244	79	64	12-0	12
Opponents	13	-	-	-		29-194	12-114	50	30	3-39	12

INTERCEPTIONS

PLAYER	NO	YARDS	AVG	TD	LNG
Craig Steltz	6	153	25.5	0	51
Chevis Jackson	4	18	4.5	0	18
Jonathan Zenon	3	42	14.0	1	24
Danny McCray	2	0	0.0	0	0
Curtis Taylor	2	22	11.0	0	22
Jacob Cutrera	1	9	9.0	0	9
Kirston Pittman	1	0	0.0	0	0
Darry Beckwith	1	0	0.0	0	0
Chad Jones	1	0	0.0	0	0
Total	21	244	11.6	1	51
Opponents	12	114	9.5	0	51

Tigers fans cheer as LSU takes the field against Mississippi State in Starkville, Miss., for the inaugural game of LSU's 2007 championship season. LSU won, 45-0.

ohio state

Leading 17-10 and facing a third-and-goal, running back Jacob Hester follows the block of tackle Ciron Black (70) and scores on a 1-yard run, much to the delight of quarterback Matt Flynn.
STAFF PHOTO BY RUSTY COSTANZA

LSU defensive tackle Ricky Jean-Francois (90), linebacker Luke Sanders (35), fullback Shawn Jordan (40) and the rest of the Tigers take the field for the title game against Ohio State.
STAFF PHOTO BY MICHAEL DeMOCKER

tigers 34
buckeyes 28

BY JAMES VARNEY STAFF WRITER

LSU capped off a second BCS championship in four years on Jan. 7, 2008, drubbing Ohio State 38-24 at the Superdome and setting off riotous jubilation among the Tigers faithful who had packed New Orleans.

The victory makes LSU the first team to win two championships in the BCS era. It also means LSU Coach Les Miles has, in three years at the helm in Baton Rouge, finished with consecutive rankings of No. 5, No. 3 and No. 1 in the country. It also adds a final, sweet win in the remarkable ledger of the year's LSU senior class, the winningest in school history.

After the game, defensive tackle Glenn Dorsey, who postponed certain riches last year in the NFL to return for his senior season, grabbed a giant LSU banner and rushed toward the band as it struck up the school's alma mater. Quarterback Matt Flynn, a fifth-year senior who was quiet and contained in the weeks leading up to the game, capped his final and only year as the starter by throwing for four touchdowns. He was voted the BCS championship game's Most Outstanding Offensive Player.

Past the confetti and the swarming on-field celebration and in the more formal surroundings of the interview room, Miles began in measured fashion to reflect on the event.

"Our senior class, it's just a lot of men that really understand how to commit to a team and fight like hell and not let any obstacle stand in its way," Miles said. "I

With the score tied at 10 in the second quarter, LSU's Darry Beckwith (48), Tyson Jackson (93) and Curtis Taylor (27) rejoice after Ricky Jean-Francois blocked a 38-yard field goal attempt by Ohio State's Ryan Pretorius.
STAFF PHOTO BY TED JACKSON

| BCS Championship | 01.07.08 | Superdome |
tigers 34 | buckeyes 28

couldn't be more proud of this team. I'm just fortunate to be the coach of the team."

He then paused, and asked to be excused for a moment as if to compose himself.

"Wahoooooo!" he exclaimed. "I just had to do that. It's just one of those things."

Such outbursts were not heard from the Ohio State side, which must now somehow recover from another championship disaster. For the second consecutive year, the Buckeyes were soundly beaten by the Southeastern Conference champion on the game's biggest stage. The loss was less lopsided than the one Florida administered (41-14) last year, and in fact Ohio State outgained the Tigers in this game.

LSU entered the game ranked just behind Ohio State. Yet oddsmakers, anticipating that LSU had the superior team in part because it played a tougher schedule than Ohio State, installed the Tigers as a four-point favorite.

By the end, LSU had blocked field-goal attempts, intercepted passes and swarmed a Buckeyes' running game that flashed some muscle and speed early in the first quarter. All told, the Tigers amassed 326 yards and converted 11 of 18 third-down attempts against an Ohio State defense that entered the game leading the NCAA in 17 categories.

LSU also overcame an early 10-0 deficit. Ohio State followed the same script it did against Florida last year by using an electrifying play to score first. This time, it was a 65-yard run by sophomore tailback Chris "Beanie" Wells, who finished with 146 rushing yards on 20 carries.

But just as it looked like LSU might be teetering — a botched snap and largely ineffective opening series — Ohio State self-destructed. A false start penalty on junior right guard Steve Rehring fatally wounded a drive that stood second-and-5 at LSU's 10-yard line. That led to a 25-yard field goal by Ryan Pretorius and, in many ways, signaled the highwater mark for the Buckeyes.

LSU, which had rallied from similar deficits this season, then poured on 24 consecutive points in 13:05 by mixing up formations to keep the Buckeyes off balance, running past Ohio State's secondary and aided along the way by four 15-yard personal foul penalties. On the other hand, LSU, which

LSU defenders Tyson Jackson (93) and Kirston Pittman (49) dislodge the ball from Ohio State quarterback Todd Boeckman in the second quarter, but the Buckeyes were able to gain possession of it.
STAFF PHOTO BY TED JACKSON

| BCS Championship | 01.07.08 | Superdome |
tigers 34 | buckeyes 28

entered the game as the second-most penalized team in the country, was not flagged for an infraction in the first half.

"We're just a stubborn team, and we don't know when to quit," Flynn said.

Miles, who could be seen trying to calm some Tigers as they came off the field on the opening possessions, said it was simply a matter of LSU finding its proper emotional pitch.

"The defense just settled down," he said. "We blocked that field goal, got a turnover on an interception and really stemmed the tide. Our defense started settling down, and they really couldn't score with us again."

It all began with 7:37 remaining in the first quarter when, facing a third-and-7, LSU got its first first down on a 10-yard pass from Flynn to senior receiver Early Doucet. That launched a 14-play, 65-yard drive that ended with a 32-yard field goal by Colt David.

LSU tied the score on an 84-yard drive on which Ohio State drew its first two personal foul calls. On a play with four receivers flanked to the right, Flynn instead threw to sophomore tight end Richard Dickson coming off the left side, and Dickson went in untouched on a 13-yard score.

It looked like Ohio State might regain the lead on its next drive, but on third down wide receiver Brian Robiskie dropped a fade pass in the end zone from quarterback Todd Boeckman, and the Buckeyes lined up for a 38-yard field-goal attempt by Pretorius. LSU defensive tackle Ricky Jean-Francois, voted the game's Most Outstanding Defensive Player, burst up the middle and batted down the attempt.

With the momentum surging toward LSU, Flynn threw his most brilliant pass of the game to give the Tigers a lead they would never relinquish. Rolling to his left on a third-and-5 at Ohio State's 10, the right-handed Flynn threw a rocket to the back left corner of the end zone, where sophomore wide receiver Brandon LaFell had beaten cornerback Malcolm Jenkins.

That play, along with a scatback run by sophomore wide receiver Trindon Holliday in which three Ohio State defenders failed to bring him down, provided the most glaring evidence that the alleged speed gap that separates Ohio State from the truly elite in college football was real, despite denials by both teams before the game.

On the Buckeyes' next possession, Boeckman faced pressure from the middle on a safety blitz by Harry Coleman, who replaced senior Craig Steltz after the All-American suffered a stinger in the second quarter. Boeckman made a desperation heave down the LSU sideline on which Chevis Jackson, whom

THE HISTORY OF THE BCS

YEAR	SUGAR BOWL	ROSE BOWL	ORANGE BOWL	FIESTA BOWL	TITLE GAME/CHAMP
2008	Georgia 41, Hawaii 10 11-2 12-1	USC 49, Illinois 17 11-2 9-4	W. Virginia 48, Oklahoma 28 11-2 11-3	Kansas 24, Va. Tech 21 12-1 11-3	**LSU** 38, Ohio St. 24 12-2 11-2
2007	**LSU** 41 | Notre Dame 14 11-2 10-3	USC 32 | Michigan 18 11-2 11-2	Louisville 24 | Wake Forest 13 12-1 11-3	Boise St. 43 | Okla. 42 13-0 11-3	Florida 41 | Ohio St. 14 13-1 12-1
2006	W. Virginia 38 | Georgia 35 11-1 10-3	Texas 41 | USC 38 13-0 12-1	Penn St. 26 | Fla. St. 23 11-1 8-5	Ohio St. 34 | Notre Dame 20 10-2 9-3	Texas
2005	Auburn 16 | Va. Tech 13 13-0 10-3	Texas 38 | Michigan 37 11-1 9-3	USC 55 | Oklahoma 19 13-0 12-1	Utah 35 | Pittsburgh 7 12-0 8-4	USC
2004	**LSU** 21 | Oklahoma 14 13-1 12-2	USC 28 | Michigan 14 12-1 10-3	Miami 16 | Fla. St. 14 11-2 10-3	Ohio St. 35 | Kansas St. 28 11-2 11-4	**LSU**
2003	Georgia 26 | Florida St. 13 13-1 9-5	Oklahoma 34 | Wash. St. 14 12-2 10-3	USC 38 | Iowa 17 11-2 11-2	Ohio St. 31 | Miami 24 14-0 12-1	Ohio St.
2002	**LSU** 47 | Illinois 34 10-3 10-2	Miami 37 | Nebraska 14 12-0 11-2	Florida 56 | Maryland 23 10-2 10-2	Oregon 38 | Colorado 16 11-1 10-3	Miami
2001	Miami 37 | Florida 20 11-1 10-3	Washington 34 | Purdue 24 11-1 8-4	Oklahoma 13 | Fla. St. 2 13-0 11-2	Oregon St. 41 | Notre Dame 9 11-1 9-3	Oklahoma
2000	Fla. St. 46 | Va. Tech 29 12-0 11-1	Wisconsin 17 | Stanford 9 10-2 8-4	Michigan 35 | Alabama 34 10-2 10-3	Nebraska 31 | Tennessee 21 12-1 9-3	Florida St.
1999	Ohio St. 24 | Texas A&M 14 11-1 11-3	Wisconsin 38 | UCLA 31 11-1 10-2	Florida 31 | Syracuse 10 10-2 8-4	Tennessee 23 | Florida St. 16 13-0 11-2	Tennessee

tigers 34 | buckeyes 28

Wells had earlier tossed aside like a dishcloth in the open field, redeemed himself with an interception that he returned 34 yards to Ohio State's 24.

Two Flynn passes advanced the ball to the 1-yard line. From there, senior tailback Jacob Hester plunged into the heart of the line three times, breaking the plane of the goal line on the last of them to stretch the lead to 24-10.

Even bigger than the gap, however, was the sensation Ohio State was once again about to be crippled by a faster, more physical SEC opponent. The sense of the game had altered permanently in the Tigers' favor, and, at halftime, Ohio State President E. Gordon Gee darted out through the back of the press box with his head down and an aide fluttering behind, trying to conceal a still-corked champagne bottle in a bucket.

Ohio State and LSU would play to the equivalent of a 14-14 tie in the second half, but the Buckeyes were mortally wounded. Their first score of the second half came on a 5-yard pass to Robiskie, and the second was a meaningless 15-yard pass from Boeckman to receiver Brian Hartline with just 1:13 remaining, the LSU side surging in ecstasy, and thunderous roars of "S-E-C! S-E-C!" washing over the hapless Ohio State bench.

In between, Ohio State did have, perhaps, one last chance to get back in the game. The Buckeyes' defense rose to the task on the opening possession of the second half, stopping LSU after an intentional grounding penalty and forcing a punt.

LSU senior punter Patrick Fisher, who kicked spectacularly all night, lined up with LSU facing fourth-and-23 from its 40-yard line. Ohio State sophomore linebacker Austin Spitler blasted through the line, however, and appeared certain to make a critical block. Not only did Spitler somehow miss the ball, he also managed to slam into Fisher. Yet another 15-yard penalty on Ohio State, and an LSU first down.

And that was that.

LSU defensive coordinator Bo Pelini, who coached his final game on the Tigers sideline and now heads to Nebraska where he will become head coach, got the first traditional Gatorade bath on the sideline from his players.

"If you're going to go out, this is the way to go out," he said. "I'm proud of this group of guys. We've been through a lot together, and I'm just excited it all came out this way."

LSU receivers Early Doucet (9) and Brandon LaFell (1) jump for joy after Doucet scampered into the end zone on a 4-yard pass from quarterback Matt Flynn.
STAFF PHOTO BY CHUCK COOK

TEAM	1ST	2ND	3RD	4TH	FINAL
LSU	**3**	**21**	**7**	**7**	**38**
Ohio State	**10**	**0**	**7**	**7**	**24**

Attendance 79,651 at the Superdome

SCORING SUMMARY

OSU — Chris Wells 65-yard run (Ryan Pretorius kick). Four plays, 77 yards in 1:26.

OSU — Pretorius 25-yard field goal. Five plays, 51 yards in 2:51.

LSU — Colt David 32-yard field goal. Fourteen plays, 65 yards in 6:51.

LSU — Richard Dickson 12-yard pass from Matt Flynn (David kick). Seven plays, 84 yards in 2:07.

LSU — Brandon LaFell 10-yard pass from Flynn (David kick). 10 plays, 66 yards in 3:28.

LSU — Jacob Hester 1-yard run (David kick). Five plays, 24 yards in 2:02.

LSU — Early Doucet 4-yard pass from Flynn (David kick). 14 plays, 80 yards in 5:56.

OSU — Brian Robiskie 5-yard pass from Todd Boeckman (Pretorius kick). Four plays, 11 yards in 2:06.

LSU — Richard Dickson 5-yard pass from Flynn (David kick). 9 plays, 53 yards in 3:53.

OSU — Brian Hartline 15-yard pass from Boeckman (Pretorius kick). Four plays, 54 yards in 0:37.

TEAM STATISTICS

TEAM STATISTICS	LSU	OHIO STATE
FIRST DOWNS	25	17
RUSHES-YARDS (NET)	49-152	30-145
PASSING YARDS	174	208
PASSES (ATT-COMP-INT)	27-19-1	26-15-2
TOTAL OFFENSE (PLAYS-YARDS)	76-326	56-353
PENALTIES (NUMBER-YARDS)	4-36	7-83
PUNTS (NUMBER-AVERAGE)	3-56.7	3-50.0
PUNT RETURNS (NUMBER-YARDS-TD)	1-8-0	1-9-0
KICKOFF RETURNS (NUMBER-YARDS-TD)	2-22-0	7-124-0
POSSESSION TIME	33:56	26:04
SACKS BY (YARDS LOST)	5-36	1-15
FIELD GOALS (ATTEMPTED-MADE)	1-1	2-1
FUMBLES-LOST	2-0	3-1

INDIVIDUAL OFFENSIVE STATISTICS

RUSHING LSU — Jacob Hester 21-86; Richard Murphy 2-33; Keiland Williams 2-20; Trindon Holliday 3-13; Matt Flynn 12-8; Early Doucet 2-7; Charles Scott 2-6; Ryan Perrilloux 1-4.
OSU — Chris Wells 20-146; Brian Hartline 1-6; Todd Boeckman 9 minus-7.

PASSING LSU — Matt Flynn 27/19-4-1, 174.
OSU — Todd Boeckman 26/15-2-2.

RECEIVING LSU — Early Doucet 7-51; Richard Dickson 4-44; Demetrius Byrd 2-28; Brandon LaFell 2-15; Keith Zinger 1-8; Charles Scott 1-16; Quinn Johnson 1-3; Keiland Williams 1 minus-1.
OSU — Brian Hartline 6-75; Brian Robiskie 5-50; Brandon Saine 3-69; Ray Small 1-14.

INDIVIDUAL DEFENSIVE STATISTICS

INTERCEPTIONS LSU — Chevis Jackson 1; Curtis Taylor 1.
OSU — Malcolm Jenkins 1.

SACKS LSU — Ali Highsmith 1.5; Glenn Dorsey 1; Tyson Jackson 1; Kirston Pittman 1; Ricky Jean-Francois 0.5.
OSU — Vernon Gholston 1.

TACKLES LSU — Ali Highsmith 8; Kirston Pittman 7; Ricky Jean-Francois 6; Curtis Taylor 5; Glenn Dorsey 5; Jonathon Zenon 4; Craig Steltz 4.
OSU — James Laurinaitis 18; Marcus Freeman 14; Kurt Coleman 10; Larry Grant 8; Donald Washington 5; Anderson Russell 5.

To the victors go the spoils, as LSU Coach Les Miles holds aloft the crystal trophy presented to the Tigers after dispatching Ohio State in the BCS championship game.
STAFF PHOTO BY CHUCK COOK

With LSU leading 31-17 in the fourth quarter, Tigers linebacker Ali Highsmith goes high to knock the ball out of the hands of Buckeyes quarterback Todd Boeckman. LSU's Harry Coleman recovered the ball, but the Tigers weren't able to capitalize.
STAFF PHOTO BY MICHAEL DEMOCKER

tigers 34 | buckeyes 28

With key plays, Tigers make it look easy

PETER FINNEY

In Tigertown, and BCS land, let's say the crystal football torch has been passed, from Nick Saban to Les Miles.

But let's make one thing clear: Four years later, Les Miles is his own man.

He's earned it.

He's paid his dues.

He's lived through a high-pressure, roller-coaster year that saw his Tigers begin the season No. 2 and finish No. 1.

He saw them counted out, once, twice, three times, but there they were Monday night, defeating the Big Ten champion 38-24 in front of 79,651, the largest crowd to see a football game in the history of the Superdome.

The Tigers won the Bowl Championship Series trophy by doing what no team came close to doing to the top-ranked Ohio State Buckeyes, by scoring 31 straight points after spotting them a 10-0 lead in the first six minutes.

They did it with big plays on both sides of the ball.

On four touchdown passes by Most Outstanding Offensive Player Matt Flynn.

On 86 hard-earned rushing yards by Jacob Hester.

On a crucial field-goal block by Ricky Jean-Francois, on a spectacular interception by Chevis Jackson.

On a fumble-forcing sack by Ali Highsmith.

They did it by getting to quarterback Todd Boeckman five times, by pressuring him into two vital interceptions, none more vital than the one by Jackson.

"I was running step for step with the receiver," Jackson said. "When I saw his eyes get bigger, I knew the ball was coming. So I turned around, and there I was."

In the fourth quarter, it was Highsmith's turn to come up with a turnaround sack that stopped a Buckeyes march.

"We were blitzing," he said, "and I was just trying to get him to throw the football. When he didn't throw it, I knocked it out of his hands. That was it."

It was the kind of evening that left the winning coach in a

With LSU leading 17-10 in the second quarter of the BCS championship game, Chevis Jackson heads upfield after intercepting a pass by Ohio State quarterback Todd Boeckman.
STAFF PHOTO ELIOT KAMENITZ

LSU's defense puts a hurt on Ohio State quarterback Todd Boeckman in the third quarter. Boeckman, who was sacked five times, completed 15 of 26 passes with two touchdowns and two interceptions.
STAFF PHOTO BY CHUCK COOK

permanent state of megawatt smiles.

"In a way," Miles said, "this was sort of like how this team has done it all year, by a bunch of guys stepping up and making the kind of plays you need to win. It was great to see how the guys settled down after that rough start. We were playing an excellent football team, and we managed to respond like champions do."

Miles felt the blocked field-goal attempt that came with OSU attempting to break a 10-10 tie was one of the biggest of the game.

table for a 25-yard field goal.

In less than six minutes, the Buckeyes had a 10-0 lead, and all the Tigers had to show was a three-and-out.

That would change when the Tigers' offense suddenly came alive and Flynn moved the team 65 yards to a field goal, a push highlighted by a couple of throws to Doucet and a 20-yard burst up the middle by Hester.

It didn't end here.

Flynn was back, this time with an 84-yard march the quarterback kept alive with a 20-yard connection to Demetrius Byrd and closed with a strike down the middle to Richard Dickson that beat a Buckeyes blitz. There was more to come.

Jean-Francois and Jackson saw to that.

After Jean-Francois went airborne to block a field-goal

> ## "In a way, this was sort of like how this team has done it all year, by a bunch of guys stepping up and making the kind of plays you need to win." LSU COACH LES MILES

For academic reasons, Jean-Francois did not become eligible until the SEC championship game against Tennessee on Dec. 1.

"The players stuck with me," he said. "Told me to keep my head up. Told me the sun was going to come up. I felt the block was real good for momentum."

Some of the finest momentum was furnished by Flynn, who completed 19 of 27 passes for 174 yards and four touchdowns.

"We grew a lot as a team this year," he said. "We turned into a stubborn team with no quit in us. We did a good job of not letting the things going on around us, the good and the bad, affect our play. When we got down early, we knew what we had to do."

As for the early moments, you can say this: Ohio State was playing like the home team, and the home team was playing like it was suffering from a severe case of the jitters.

A minute and a half into the game, Chris Wells was slicing off tackles and taking off on a 65-yard touchdown gallop, the longest of the season for the Buckeyes. He was hardly touched.

Wide receiver Early Doucet bobbled a short pass in the flat.

A bad snap from the shotgun formation sent Flynn in reverse, chasing the ball back to his 6-yard line.

A blown assignment in the Tigers' secondary resulted in a wide-open Brandon Saine grabbing a 44-yard pass that set the

attempt, Flynn took the Tigers 55 yards, hitting passes inside and outside, finally nailing Brandon LaFell on a 10-yard beauty that came on third-and-5.

Three plays later, it was Jackson running stride-for-stride with Ray Small, turning and picking off a Boeckman rainbow at the LSU 42 and running it back to the Buckeyes' 24.

Five plays later, it was Hester nudging it in from the 1 and another third-down conversion.

The Tigers had a 24-10 lead.

The Tigers had converted on eight of their last nine third-down attempts.

The most penalized team in the SEC, one that averaged 10 a game, had played for 30 minutes with zero flags.

For 60 minutes, they would play well enough to win a national championship.

When he had dried out from a postgame soaking, when the confetti had stopped dropping, Miles had just a few simple sentences to sum things up.

"We're a deserving champion. We are a no 'I' champion. We are a 'we' champion.

"That's the best kind."

the tigers

ROSTER

#	NAME	POS	HT	WT	CL	HOMETOWN
1	Brandon LaFell	WR	6-3	205	So.	Houston
2	Demetrius Byrd	WR	6-2	195	Jr.	Miami
2	Orlando Gunn	DB	5-7	179	Fr.	Harker Heights, Texas
3	Chad Jones	S	6-3	218	Fr.	Baton Rouge
4	Ryan Anders	K	5-6	207	Fr.	Baton Rouge
4	Jai Eugene	CB	5-11	184	Fr.	St. Rose
5	Chad Moody	DB	5-11	187	So.	Baton Rouge
5	Keiland Williams	RB	6-0	226	So.	Lafayette
6	Colt David	PK	5-9	173	Jr.	Grapevine, Texas
6	Joey Stutson	RB	5-10	202	So.	Mandeville
7	Ali Highsmith	LB	6-1	223	Sr.	Miami
8	Trindon Holliday	WR	5-5	160	So.	Zachary
9	Early Doucet	WR	6-1	210	Sr.	St. Martinville
10	Ricky Dixon	WR	6-2	210	Fr.	LaPlace
10	Josh Graham	PK	5-10	172	So.	Covington
11	Ryan Perrilloux	QB	6-3	227	So.	LaPlace
11	Kelvin Sheppard	LB	6-3	223	Fr.	Stone Mountain, Ga.
12	Quentin LeDay	WR	6-2	193	Jr.	Opelousas
12	Jarrett Lee	QB	6-2	211	Fr.	Brenham, Texas
13	Donnie Chaucer	DB	5-11	190	Sr.	Hammond
13	Jimmy Welker	QB	6-3	223	Sr.	Tarzana, Calif.
14	Ron Brooks	DB	5-11	171	Fr.	Irving, Texas
14	Andrew Hatch	QB	6-3	214	So.	Henderson, Nevada
15	Matt Flynn	QB	6-3	227	Sr.	Tyler, Texas
16	Craig Steltz	S	6-2	209	Sr.	New Orleans
17	Shomari Clemons	S	6-1	217	Fr.	West Monroe
17	T.C. McCartney	QB	6-3	202	Fr.	Boulder, Colo.
18	Jacob Hester	FB	6-0	224	Sr.	Shreveport
19	Jonathan Zenon	CB	6-0	180	Sr.	Breaux Bridge
21	Chevis Jackson	CB	6-0	184	Sr.	Mobile, Ala.
22	Jeremy Bunting	WR	6-0	182	Jr.	Tioga
23	Stefoin Francois	DB	6-1	207	Fr.	Reserve
23	Josh McManus	WR	5-11	192	Sr.	New Orleans
24	Harry Coleman	S	6-2	205	So.	Baldwin
25	Brady Glaser	WR	5-11	191	Fr.	Dry Creek
25	Phelon Jones	DB	5-11	195	Fr.	Mobile, Ala.
26	Richard Murphy	RB	6-1	197	Fr.	Rayville
27	August Mangin	WR	5-11	185	So.	Lewisville, Texas
27	Curtis Taylor	S	6-3	200	Jr	Franklinton
28	R.J. Jackson	RB	6-0	205	So	Houston
28	Joe Maltempi	DB	5-8	166	So.	Chester, Va.
29	Chris Hawkins	DB	6-1	175	So.	Walker
30	Chad Baniecki	FB	6-1	226	Jr.	Seton, Ariz.
30	Josh Jasper	PK/P	5-10	155	Fr.	Memphis, Tenn.
31	John Williams	CB	5-11	180	Fr.	Breaux Bridge
32	Charles Scott	RB	5-11	226	So.	Saline
33	Tyson Andrus	DB	6-0	170	So.	Lafayette
33	Adam McClure	WR	6-0	177	Fr.	Baton Rouge
34	Stevan Ridley	FB	6-0	221	Fr.	Natchez, Miss.
35	Luke Sanders	LB	6-5	242	Sr.	West Monroe
36	Patrick Fisher	P	6-5	238	Fr.	Hyattsville, Md.
37	Paul Felio	LB	6-0	221	Fr.	League City, Texas
37	Phillip Pigott	RB	6-0	216	Jr.	Pearl River
38	Brady Dalfrey	P	6-0	206	Jr.	Carencro
38	Anthony Zehyoue	DE	6-1	270	Sr.	Baton Rouge
39	Caleb Angelle	DE	6-5	230	Sr.	Breaux Bridge
39	Andrew Crutchfield	PK/P	5-11	190	Fr.	Concord, N.C.
40	Shawn Jordan	FB	5-11	254	Sr.	El Paso, Texas
41	Jordon Corbin	TE	6-4	240	Fr.	Lakeland, Fla.
42	R.J. Gillen	WR	6-0	187	Fr.	Memphis, Tenn.

ROSTER

#	NAME	POS	HT	WT	CL	HOMETOWN
43	Blake Nichols	LB	6-0	231	Fr.	Metairie
43	Lydell Smith	LB	5-10	208	Fr.	Shreveport
44	Daniel Graff	DB	5-11	175	Fr.	Metairie
44	Danny McCray	S	6-1	206	So.	Houston
45	Quinn Johnson	FB	6-2	238	Jr.	Edgard
46	J.D. Lott	TE	6-4	227	Fr.	Hoover, Ala.
47	Tremaine Johnson	DE	6-2	282	Jr.	Galena Park, Texas
48	Darry Beckwith	LB	6-1	230	Jr.	Baton Rouge
49	Kirston Pittman	DE	6-4	252	Sr.	Garyville
50	Joey Crappell	SNP	6-2	214	Fr.	Patterson
50	Micah Metrailer	LB	6-1	237	So.	Baton Rouge
51	Zachary Midulla	LB	5-8	187	Fr.	Brandon, Fla.
51	Jacob O'Hair	SNP	6-2	237	Sr.	Rancho Cucamonga, Calif.
52	Ace Foyil	LB	6-3	230	So.	Madisonville
53	T-Bob Hebert	C	6-3	277	Fr.	Norcross, Ga.
53	Jonathan Nixon	LB	6-2	257	So.	Little Rock, Ark.
54	Jacob Cutrera	LB	6-4	235	So.	Lafayette
55	Andrew Decker	OL	6-3	280	Jr.	Holland, Ohio
56	Perry Riley	LB	6-1	232	So.	Ellenwood, Ga.
57	Richard Dugas	C	6-1	280	Fr.	Lincoln, Neb.
59	Cole Louviere	OL	6-5	291	Sr.	River Ridge
61	Trey Helms	OL	6-4	261	Fr.	Stuttgart, Ark.
62	Robert Smith	OL	6-2	273	Jr.	Bossier City
63	Ryan Miller	C	6-6	302	Jr.	Lake Charles
64	Matt Allen	OL	6-3	265	Fr.	Spring, Texas
65	Lyle Hitt	OG	6-2	299	So.	Baton Rouge
66	Max Holmes	OL	6-4		So.	Baton Rouge
67	Mark Snyder	OL	6-7	291	Fr.	Kenner
68	Josh Dworaczyk	OL	6-6	280	Fr.	New Iberia
69	Sean Gaudet	PK	5-9	166	Jr	New Orleans
70	Ciron Black	OT	6-5	320	So.	Tyler, Texas
71	Carnell Stewart	OT	6-5	320	So.	River Ridge
72	Glenn Dorsey	DT	6-2	303	Sr.	Gonzales
73	Will Arnold	OL	6-5	330	Sr.	Gloster, Miss.
74	Brett Helms	C	6-2	270	Jr.	Stuttgart, Ark.
76	Jarvis Jones	OL	6-7	294	Fr.	Rosenburg, Texas
77	Ernest McCoy	OL	6-5	320	Fr.	Belle Glade, Fla.
78	Joseph Barksdale	OL	6-4	310	Fr.	Detroit
79	Herman Johnson	OL	6-7	356	Jr.	Olla
80	Terrance Toliver	WR	6-5	190	Fr.	Hempstead, Texas
81	Mit Cole	TE	6-4	260	Sr.	Picayune, Miss.
82	Richard Dickson	TE	6-3	235	So.	Ocean Springs, Miss.
83	Mitch Joseph	TE	6-3	243	Fr.	New Iberia
84	Rahim Alem	DE	6-3	254	So	New Orleans
85	Alex Russian	TE	6-5	226	Fr.	Round Rock, Texas
86	Chris Mitchell	WR	6-0	180	So.	Marrero
87	Jared Mitchell	WR	5-11	198	So.	New Iberia
88	Donald Hains	DL	5-11	243	Sr.	Diamondhead, Miss.
88	Ian Harding	WR	6-1	196	Fr.	New Orleans
89	Keith Zinger	TE	6-4	250	Sr.	Leesville
90	Ricky Jean-Francois	DE	6-3	281	So	Miami
91	Charles Alexander	DT	6-3	292	Jr.	Breaux Bridge
92	Drake Nevis	DL	6-1	288	Fr.	Marrero
93	Tyson Jackson	DE	6-5	291	Jr.	Edgard
94	Will Blackwell	DE	6-4	297	Fr.	West Monroe
95	Lazarius Levingston	DE	6-4	277	Fr.	Ruston
96	Kentravis Aubrey	DL	6-3	285	Fr.	Bastrop
97	Al Woods	DT	6-4	316	So.	Elton
98	Sidell Corley	DE	6-4	274	Fr.	Mobile, Ala.
98	Trent Hebert	PK	5-9	182	Fr.	Cecilia
99	Marlon Favorite	DT	6-1	302	Jr.	Harvey

STATISTICS

CATEGORY	LSU	OPPONENT
Attendance	722,166	333,039
Games-avg. per game	8-90,271	5-66,608
Scoring	503	255
Points per game	38.7	19.6
First downs	291	214
Rushing	141	79
Passing	137	110
Penalty	13	25
Rushing yardage	2,846	1,340
Yards gained rushing	3,182	1,719
Yards lost rushing	336	379
Carries	563	434
Average per carry	5.1	3.1
Average per game	218.9	103.1
Touchdowns rushing	34	13
Passing yardage	2,980	2,350
Att.-Comp.-Int.	415-237-12	425-197-21
Average per pass	7.2	5.5
Average per catch	12.6	11.9
Average per game	229.2	180.8
Touchdowns passing	25	17
Total offense	5,826	3,690
Total plays	978	859
Average per play	6.0	4.3
Average per game	448.2	283.8
Kick returns (No.-yds)	40-805	87-1785
Punt returns (No.-yds)	22-128	21-199
Int. returns (No.-yds)	21-244	12-114
Kick return average	20.1	20.5
Punt return average	5.8	9.5
INT return average	11.6	9.5
Fumbles-lost	16-3	23-12
Penalties-yards	113-844	60-483
Punts-yards	58-2,519	79-3,093
Average per punt	43.4	39.2
Net punt average	35.5	36.5
Time of possession*	32:07	27:53
Third-down conversions	93/205	68/189
Third-down percentage	45%	36%
Fourth-down conversions	12/15	4/18
Fourth-down percentage	80%	22%
Sacks by-yards	32-246	29-194
Touchdowns scored	61	32
Field goals-attempts	25-32	10-12
On-side kicks	0-0	0-3
Red-zone scores	64-69	30-35
Red-zone TD	44-69	22-35
Extra-point attempts	58-58	29-30

*per game